"I knew Paula Sager's father Bob as the wise, humble, and scrupulous man who loved his family and country and was generous to both. Paula's memoir, beginning with a wristwatch and ending with a swan, reveals the extraordinary experience they shared after he became sick. Time disappears; their reality becomes mysteriously and beautifully something known only to the two of them. As the horizon beckons her father onward, Paula achieves a clarity about life, death, and love and an affirmation that "all earthly beings are participating in something vastly larger and more intertwined than any of us can fathom." This memoir holds a powerful message for the reader; I've already started my second round."

— Bill Moyers, journalist and public commentator

"In this luminous meditation on the death of a beloved parent, Paula Sager gracefully dances between embodiment and contemplation, between heartbreak and gratitude, between memory and presence. Her vivid depictions of lives being fully lived, from kayaking the Atlantic waters to shopping for a watch in a suburban mall, make this book sing, and render her father's dying a holy, holy thing."

— Mirabai Starr, author of *Wild Mercy* and *Ordinary Mysticism*

"This quiet and shimmering memoir of loss and love reminds those of us who practice medicine that the process of dying is not only corporal but also spiritual, and to ignore the latter is to miss our deep commitment to and the honor of accompanying the patient through a time of great loneliness."

— Michael D. Stein, author of *Accidental Kindness: A Doctor's Notes on Empathy*

"*The Watch* is a tender and beautifully written account of the author's relationship with her father, and the time leading up to and following his death. Paula Sager seamlessly weaves the threads of loving connection, intimate glimpses of family life, childhood memories, and contemplations on the complex of feelings evoked during this momentous time.

Moving with grace between the gnarly realities of dealing with cancer in the family, and a wider perspective that embraces past and future within the present, Sager is "left with a clear knowing: *Now is the time to savor being in this body, in this life.*" This book is indeed a celebration of life lived to the full, moment by moment, even as it traces the path of grief at the loss of a loved one."

— Linda Hartley, author of *Wisdom of the Body Moving* and *Embodied Spirit, Conscious Earth.*

"I am in love with Paula Sager's questions: *Can you be present enough for this? And this? What supports you in being present? How do we say goodbye to those who are leaving our known world? How do we stay connected to those who leave?* This thoughtful memoir invites us to bring such wonderment into our own bodies, to be curious about our own relationships with our beloveds, with time, with mortality. It is not easy to be wrestled by unanswerable questions, but as Paula's father would say, "That's the beauty of it." And this is a beautiful telling, a sacred endeavor exploring the thresholds of birth and death, what comes before, what comes after, and that most difficult and most glorious betweenness we call now."

— Rosemerry Wahtola Trommer, author of *The Unfolding* and host of The Poetic Path

"With intimate storytelling and philosophical depth, Paula Sager offers a poignant exploration of life's deepest truths revealing how the journey of one can catalyze change in us all. *The Watch* is more than a book—it's an invitation to pause, to feel deeply, and to experience love, loss, and our shared humanity with fresh eyes and an open heart."

— Lisa Napora, PhD, founding director of The Mindfulness Alliance and WeShift Institute facilitator

"While offering glimpses into her deeply personal experiences with loss, grief and growth, Paula Sager gives readers the space and inspiration to reflect upon their own mysterious relationship to time and to their loved ones. You will be comforted and moved by Paula's open-hearted revelations large and small."

— Priscilla Warner, author of New York Times bestsellers, *The Faith Club* and *Learning to Breathe*

"With *The Watch*, Paula Sager takes the reader on a deep dive into the mysteries of memory and intuition, exploring what it means to be human, and what it means to love another. Beautifully written and deeply wise, this is a story we can all learn from."
— Elizabeth Shick, author of *The Golden Land,* winner of the AWP Prize for the Novel

"Paula Sager writes that finding a book feels like being found. The Watch will find all of us who contemplate the passage of time and the persistence of love for those present and not. This beautiful book doesn't give us the answers, but instead offers us enormous consolation in the gifts of our own insight and wonder."
— Hester Kaplan, author of *The Edge of Marriage* and winner of the Flannery O'Connor Award for short fiction

"*The Watch* is a deep and personal inquiry into grief, love, and the nature of consciousness. Paula Sager's intimate narrative evokes the wise presence of her late father in ways that feel like a real encounter, bringing the reader into close contact with the mystery of relationship. As the interplay of life and death unfolds, we receive glimpses of timelessness and encounter the numinous. This is a beautiful, spacious and evocative read. A celebration of the fullness of life, where everyday details become portals to universal questions."
– Anne Egseth, author of *This is All He Asks of You*

The

TIME TO WITNESS THE BEAUTY OF IT ALL

Watch

Paula Sager

Design by Melody Stanford Martin

Published by Wildhouse Publications, an imprint of Wildhouse Publishing
(www.wildhousepublishing.com). No part of this book may be reproduced
in any manner without the written permission from the publisher, except
in brief quotations embodied in critical articles or reviews. Contact info@
wildhousepublishing.com.

Print ISBN: 978-1-961741-17-1
eBook ISBN: 978-1-961741-21-8

For Theo, Savanna, Colton, Sienna, Arya,
and others still to come

Contents

I am who I am because of you, whoever you are...
what else can we do but dare to try to be more truthful,
so we can see ourselves in each other more clearly?

— Janet Adler

BEFORE

A book tells a story, a watch tells time. What happens when the watch stops? Or the phone rings and life as you know it changes forever?

Perhaps you've had such surreal moments. Maybe you've wondered how on earth you would manage to get through some seemingly impossible situation. Maybe you're facing such challenges right now. Even in the midst of unnerving uncertainty, you may have a sense that life's most difficult passages can be times of profound insight, growth, beauty, and love. Or life can simply crush us.

When my father was diagnosed with cancer, the ground beneath my feet seemed to fall away. As he faced the upending of his life, I felt woefully ill-equipped to offer support to the person who had always been the center of gravity within our family. Somehow I would need to find my own grounding while keeping aloft the already precarious juggling act of my life. Surprisingly, my training as a dancer—along with years of studying contemplative practices—had prepared me better than I could have imagined. My time studying the Discipline of Authentic Movement with its founder, Janet Adler, had led me precisely to this crossroad where the intersection of my practice and my life was undeniable. Throughout my father's illness, when I felt myself stretched beyond what I could bear, I silently repeated a phrase I had learned from Janet: *May I be present enough.*

To be present enough with my father, I would need to dig deep—into resources I scarcely knew I had, into a level of awareness that resides within us all.

Looking inward, to a time long before the doctors detected cancer in my father's body, I can see myself as a quiet, earnest young girl sitting cross-legged with the other children on a brown nubby rug. The woman in the large rocking chair leans forward as she reads aloud from *Little Tim and the Brave Sea Captain*.[1] Her voice is warm and steady. She doesn't dramatize the story, she simply tells it, turning the pages of the book, one at a time, a fluid, mesmerizing rhythm. The words, even more than the pictures, pour into me. I am in a vast liquid realm of time and space.

When the story is done, the woman closes the book. Now it is time to find our own books. "You can pick four to take home with you," she says, rising out of her chair.

Moving among the illustrated books on display, I discover that finding a book feels like being found. The decision comes swiftly each time as, one by one, the four reveal themselves to me. From this distance, decades later, I recognize this way of knowing as immediate and intuitive.

The weekly ritual of Saturday morning at the library provided experiences that were vivid and intimately my own. I felt close to myself, at home in the collaborative hush of people in room after room of books. I loved having permission and freedom to seek, not knowing where the quest would take me. That a book calls to me—then and now—is an exhilarating moment of recognition. It's an intuitive hunch that someone else's story might in some way bring me closer to my own story.

Despite their enormous variety, all of our stories share the two experiences we know the least about: our birth and our death. Most of us, at some point in our lives, will also experience the death of a loved one, sometimes more often than feels fair. All of us, each one of us, carry some form of suffering: anguish for what has happened in our lives, fear for what may happen, longing for what may never happen. Janet Adler writes:

> There is suffering seen and not seen, heard and not heard all the time everywhere, everywhere. Suffering caused by nature, by fellow humans, by invisible and mysterious forces. Suffering exists for each one coming and going, one by one, the one coming, the one going. Each one turns or does not turn into the suffering, grows or does not grow, recovers or does not recover. Completely subjective, comparison is meaningless.[2]

For thirty years I studied with Janet, learning to practice and then teach the Discipline of Authentic Movement, which is both an approach to embodied awareness and a path toward witness consciousness.[3] Experiencing the discipline for the first time in the early 1990s, I felt a sense of homecoming, something rediscovered: permission and freedom to seek, not knowing where the quest would take me. Coming closer to myself.

From Janet, I learned that if I close my eyes and attend to if and how my body wants to move, something meaningful happens, and that having an outer witness to the process profoundly deepens the experience. Authentic Movement is a practice grounded in relationship: *When you see me with compassion, as I am, I can see myself more clearly.* An awakened presence of the *inner* witness begins to develop.

When we are seen enough, when we can see ourselves with compassion and greater awareness of the way our minds produce the judgments and projections that cloud our vision, we may find it possible to see someone else more clearly, as they are. Our differences, including our physical bodies, our sensations, our emotions, our dreams, our images and memories, our languages and cultures, become infinite details to be discovered, to be cherished.

Someone is born, someone dies. Here lives the ineffable. As soon as I write these two words—*birth, death*—I am at the threshold of the unknown. What is here? What can I know in the vastness of so much mystery?

My hands turn over, palms facing up, my arms slowly opening to either side.

I can know this gesture.

Fingers tingle, palms empty.

I can know these sensations.

My heart is full, emotions tumbling, changing.

I can know these feelings of fear, awe, dread, confusion, joy, numbness, grief. When so very much is unknown, my body is a doorway into knowing something that is present and true in this moment.

A doorway to the inner witness. The closing of eyes and turning of attention to feelings, sensations, and impulses in one's body allows inner experience to become active and palpable.

The Watch invites you to witness your own experiences, discovering what wants to be felt and known within the mysteries of life, death, and time. At the end of each chapter, you will find a few contemplative words. Space within the flow of reading to meet the present moment and drop beneath story into the realm of experience. You can choose how you want to use these words. When it comes to engaging one's own inner experience, choice is essential. You might read these short verses and stay with whatever arises within you. You might skip over them and return to them later. Or you might decide to cover my words with a scrap of white paper so the page becomes an empty canvas where your very own personal portal may appear. Everything is welcome.

I sincerely hope that as I hold my story up to the light, it bears witness to your life's stories in ways that help you *be present enough* when it matters most.

Paula Sager

ONE

One week after my father died, the hands and numbers began falling off my watch. It was the kind of watch that shows every third number—3, 6, 9, 12—so at first it was disorienting, seeing an empty space where the six had been. I didn't realize what was missing and just stared at the pearly absence of the lower half, the image now a face without a mouth.

A few days later, the nine and the second hand took flight. A day later, the three. Still, the watch continued to tell time until one night it stopped at five past eleven. I discovered this the next morning when I put my watch on and found the six wedged in the V-shaped crook of the little and big hands. The spontaneous disassembling of the watch was a startling and perplexing sign. What was I to make of it?

My father always wore a watch. Waterproof was essential so he could keep it on while swimming and kayaking, two of his favorite pastimes. When his watch broke one early spring day, he was eager to replace it right away. But there were always more pressing matters like doctor appointments, pill and meal regimens, daily walks, and rest. Time was no longer his time the way it was before he became sick.

A few weeks after my father's watch stopped working, I drove from Rhode Island to Connecticut to my parents' place in Stamford, less than an hour outside of New York City. It's a home I've only visited as their adult child, where they moved as my youngest brother was finishing his final year of high school.

I had agreed to spend a week with my father at my parents' home while my mother was away on a trip. Within minutes of my mother's departure, my father pointed to my wrist.

"I like the watch you're wearing," he said. "Let's go find one like it for me."

1

My watch, with its four visible numbers, had an oversized, silver-rimmed, round face and a thin black leather wristband. It was a semi-cool update on the classic Timex, slightly more feminine in a way I liked. At the sprawling local mall, black-strapped and simple wasn't easy to find. All the watches in the department stores were big, shiny, and expensive. After walking the mall from end to end, we found a tiny store called Time Zone tucked into a far corner on the third floor. Even there, with a wider selection of casual options, my father couldn't find exactly what he had in mind. He settled for a no-nonsense Swiss Army brand with a dark brown strap. Not what he had wanted but *good enough*—or so I'd thought.

At the end of the week, as we sat outside enjoying a soft, warm breeze and watching the slow drift of clouds over Long Island Sound, I sensed my father staring at my arm.

"I really like your watch," he said. He did not need to add, "Better than mine."

Not knowing what else to say, I suggested that we trade. He could wear my watch, and I would wear his.

"Okay," he said, without any hesitation.

We each took off our watch. I put his on my left wrist and then helped him fasten mine on his left wrist. We then resumed gazing at the water. Our exchange felt like a wordless pact, even though I had no idea what I was agreeing to.

My father had an expansive relationship with time. When I was growing up in Toronto, I don't remember that he ever brought home or even talked about his office work. Home was where he was free to develop his passions like listening to music or playing the piano, especially jazz, and most especially his slow-thumping take on Thelonious Monk. And he loved to cook.

Sometimes at night during the week, he read Northern Italian cookbooks and planned ambitious meals. Frequently on Saturday mornings, I woke up early and went with him to meet the farmers and shopkeepers displaying their wares at St. Lawrence Market. With a week's worth of fresh produce and unusual meats and cheeses, he'd be back home to start the process of commandeering the kitchen, happily peeling, chopping, marinating, and sautéing. All of which gave my mother, the artist, time to paint.

With dinner roasting or at a low simmer, my father would often join my three younger brothers—John, Jeff, and Ben—and me in whichever sport was in season: touch football in the fall, ice hockey in the winter, softball and tennis in the spring and summer. My father had been a swimmer in high school and college and had an athletic ease when it came to sports except, most notably, hockey. For many years, my family lived around the corner from our elementary school, and every December, someone would show up with a snowplow to clear a big rectangle on the north side of the schoolyard. Someone else would follow, spraying water into the snow-embanked oblong, returning day after day until the surface was smooth and thick enough to last the winter. We never knew who the rink-makers were, but my brothers and I eagerly looked forward to their arrival each year. We would spend hours at the schoolyard, playing neighborhood pick-up hockey, or just noodling around on the ice.

My father could be counted on to make an occasional appearance. After a less than successful attempt to learn to skate, and many bruised hips later, he would forgo skates and step in as goalie for whichever team was winning. Even with boots, it was always a short yet treacherous trek as he made his way off the ice to the snow-packed surface of the playground and back home to finish cooking dinner.

It was nearly dark when my brothers and I would return home with a clatter of hockey sticks and skates. The dank smell of wet woolen hats, socks, and mittens blended with a synesthesia of sound, aroma, and warmth. With dinner ready, my father would usually be found at the piano working out the chord changes of a Monk tune.

Living in Toronto in the 1960's and 70's, it seemed there was an infinite reservoir of time for my father to do the things he liked to do. Years later, when my own children were growing up, in spite of my best intentions and my father's example, I often worked in the evenings and on weekends. I could only rarely shake the feeling that I was racing against time. A held-breath sensation of binding constriction accompanied the never-enough-time voice in my head.

There is something so primal about how we inhabit sequential time. I can barely have a thought without some reference to *now, then, soon, when, before, after, tomorrow, yesterday, someday, next*, or *never*. Language is our compass as we navigate the continuum of time. Yet, for much of my life, awareness of time has provoked an undertow of anxiety within me; a fear of not knowing what is coming next mixed with the fear of not knowing when it will all end. I know a day will come when time will go on without me.

One antidote I've found for these particular fears is acceptance of the reality of *not knowing*. To intentionally inhabit this state can take the distressing edge off such feelings. When I close my eyes and the visible world disappears, I am closing my eyes to the illusion that I know exactly where I am and where I'm going. When we close our eyes in the presence of a witness—perhaps a trusted other, or nature, or even a poem that deeply touches us—our not knowing may open us to an inner experience unfolding. In her acceptance of the Nobel Prize in Literature, the poet Wisława Szymborska spoke of inspiration being born from a continuous "I don't know." The reason she so greatly values this "little phrase," Szymborska says, is because "It's small, but it flies on mighty wings. It expands our lives to include the spaces within us as well as those outer expanses in which our tiny earth hangs suspended."[4]

Practicing meditation and body-based disciplines have led me to ways of being that seemed to come so naturally to my father. He had, what appeared to me, an unusual degree of tolerance for and openness to not knowing. Along with his expansive sense of time, my father lived by a warm and inclusive moral code exemplified by two mantric lines. The first, *we're all on the same side*, was a phrase that could apply to a family squabble, a business deal, or even a global conflict. His use of it seemed to suggest not that we're all in agreement, but that we're all looking at the same thing from different perspectives.

His second favorite phrase, *that's the beauty of it*, was his invariable response to something you normally wouldn't like or want to do. The enthusiastic pitch of his voice was his good-humored yet emphatic way of nudging my brothers and me to expand our outlook in some way. This often involved some less than appealing chore we were supposed to do or something he was cooking that we thought was disgusting. In response to our protests to being forced to eat meals involving the pink squishy meat-blobs on his kitchen cutting board, he would cheerily reply, "But it's sheep pancreas. And that's the beauty of it!"

The very reason you thought something was unappetizing was the very reason it apparently was something to marvel at and enjoy. This was his kind of teaching. Nothing dogmatic, just positivity and enthusiasm for a dish of food we thought looked offensive or for an idea that was new and untried. Much later in life, I learned that the refrains we'd heard so often at home had played a part in the navigation of his professional career.

An old photo shows me and my father in the basement apartment where my parents and I lived when we first moved to Canada, before my brothers were born. In the black-and-white image, my father and I are standing in a corner of the living room, unaware that a picture is being taken.

My father was about twenty-eight years old at the time, a year or two into his job as a junior insurance broker in Toronto. Just five years earlier, he was in El Paso, TX, stationed in the Army. While on a brief leave, he returned home for the holidays. It was a cold late December day in Chicago when, with minimal fanfare, my parents married. On the return trip to El Paso my mother joined my father. Within a year of living on the army base, they were on their way to New York City, where my father had found an underwriting job at the Royal Globe Insurance Company and my mother was hired by the marketing department.

In the photo, I see my father wearing loose-fitting pants, a striped open-neck sweater, and black socks without shoes. He is looking down with a calm focus; his hands are open, ready to catch the ball that I've thrown up to him. I am about three years old, wearing scuffed saddle shoes, black tights, and a short dress. The ball has just left my hands: my head is thrown back, my arms still overhead, wrists softly flung forward.

Somehow my mother captured that moment of the exchange, when the ball hangs motionless between being thrown and being caught. Looking at the photo now, I see the ball hovering in the empty space between me and my father. My breath catches. I'm overcome with a sense that something continues between us to this day. Like my experience with the spontaneous disassembling face of the watch, I don't know what this means, but I do know it holds meaning. The talismanic qualities of this photo and the watch my father and I shared belong to the same emptiness: a space where the story is not over.

Again and again, my mind revisits moments with my father during the last eighteen months of his life. Words, scenes, and images return like echoes. I don't know why some memories come readily and others have grown dim. Or why, during the time he was sick, I recorded some experiences in my journal and not others. Much of what I wrote seemed incidental at the time. But now I find myself looking at the sequence of entries as a chronological stream, a river I want to swim in and sometimes step back from, hoping I might see something in the shape and meander that wasn't visible in the day-to-day motion of life in the living of it.

A book by John Berger titled *Bento's Sketchbook* has a subtitle that's a question: *How does the impulse to draw something begin?* The word *impulse* jumps at me and mingles with my own curiosity and attraction to it. An impulse stands for something mysterious and inner, something that arises unseen and unbidden, only to manifest as our very being in action.

Berger's drawings are of people and things he encounters in his life: a blooming iris, a dried fig, seed pods of a poppy plant, a bicycle, faces of friends or people he has met, his right hand drawn by his left, an empty chair. For weeks at a time, he carries his sketchbook with him, unopened—"all the while we are observing things without feeling the compulsion to draw them," until, he writes, "suddenly it happens. We have to draw this."[5]

Why, out of the flow of days and weeks, out of everything that happened in my life during the time my father was sick, why do I return to certain moments? Why do some of these moments open, like a portal, to childhood memories and to my deepest questions and longings?

Near the end of *Bento's Sketchbook*, Berger offers a possible answer. Where he writes *drawn* and *drawings,* I fill in my own words, *written* and *writings:*

> There is a symbiotic desire to get closer and closer, to enter the self of what is being drawn, and simultaneously, there

is the foreknowledge of immanent distance. Such drawings
aspire to be both a secret rendezvous and an au revoir![6]

Yearning for nearness, the awareness of distance, and this strange
phrase: symbiotic desire. Yes, the impulse arises out of relationship. If
it is symbiotic—a mutually beneficial relationship—then the mystery
only deepens. The story of *The Watch* tracks a journey inward, following
a daughter's impulse to reach across an impossible span of distance to
find her father. It's both secret rendezvous and au revoir.

Impulse
hidden within longing—
welcome
to the threshold
of not knowing

Two

The phone call comes on a cold day in January with the news that my father has a mass, a growth, something "serious" and "not good" at the base of his esophagus. So the dreaded words are here along with an instant numbness, and an inner voice that says *be strong*.

What does healing look like now? I think of all the somatic and contemplative practices I've studied and taught over the years. I think of all that my mother—the woman who was there to support the birth of almost every one of her twelve grandchildren—knows about food, healing, and meditation. And still, what do we know about what my father needs—his particular body, his mind, his spirit? What does healing look like for him? And where does one begin?

For days the numbness continues. I feel suspended in a familiar, hard-to-breathe state of not knowing what's next. A week of delayed reports and unresponsive doctors leaves us with nothing to go on. After my father has a more in-depth endoscopic procedure, my brother Jeff calls with the update. He speaks slowly. The information comes in small bits.

"There is a tumor. It extends down along the lower esophagus. On the right. Spreading wide at the base and slightly beyond. Into the stomach area."

I hang up the phone, unable to move, frozen. As I imagine the tumor, my hands tighten, becoming closed fists. My mouth wants to open wide, but no sound comes. I stay with this silent urge to scream for a long time, all the way to something else. Surrender. A feeling arises of falling backwards, only to be caught and held in the arms of Love.

This is how it begins, states of dread and fear alternating with a kind of raw faith and willingness to surrender to love and hope.

On the morning of Barack Obama's first inauguration, I wake up early. In the deep blue dark of dawn, I see a crescent of light, a sideways cup of possibility hanging in the silence of a new morning.

A few days later I drive to Stamford, Connecticut to see my father and meet up with Molly, my oldest child and the first born of the grandchildren. She is going to spend a semester abroad, and I will be joining her for a week at the outset. We'll stop in Paris to visit my brother John and his family and celebrate Molly's twenty-first birthday. Then on to Rome, where she and I will explore the city for a couple of days before her program begins.

When I arrive at my parents' house, there is a palpable sense of purpose and optimism. My mother is a force of nature. She has helped friends of hers through cancer; she knows the foods that support healing and those that don't. Molly and I join her in doing everything in our power to deter a downward turn in my father's health.

Much later, in one of his desk drawers, we find my father's own words of positive intention in a short, handwritten letter to himself:

> Bob—
> You can do this—
> Be generous, humorous, deeply supportive of all
> these fine people.
> Be unself-conscious & take good care of your body.
> Take all the help you can get.
>
> OK OK

I ponder the inflection behind those last two words. Was he cheering himself on? Maybe. My father wrote many letters to friends, family, and colleagues, but he was not a diarist. In this context, the words, *OK OK*, bear his slight impatience with anything that might be construed as self-analysis. While he could be as perceptive about himself as he was about others, inward reflections were not something he was inclined to spend much time documenting.

His letter-to-self reminded me of the only email I ever received from him. He had no interest in having or using a computer; his messages to the world were, for the most part, handwritten or sent electronically by an assistant or on rare occasions, as in this instance, typed by him on my mother's computer. His email referred to a message I had sent to all the adult members of the family in which I suggested that we might generate some new thoughts on a situation we were dealing with by meditating on it. My father's response came later that day and included the following:

> I read your email (after Mom printed me a copy) with great interest. Then I did my best to empty my head for 15 minutes as you suggested. This has worked incredibly well for me twice in the past when I had to speak eulogies at funerals and discovered that thinking about them was worse than no help at all.

After sharing the thought that came to him, he continued:

> That was it. Then I was unable to prevent myself from beginning to entertain once again destructive thoughts.

> Love, Dad

I don't know to what degree my father was consciously distinguishing between two kinds of thinking. One, an unproductive, even destructive way of thinking and the other, a receptive state of mind in which creative and productive thoughts can arise. His intuitive capacity to generate original thoughts was highly developed, but again, it wasn't a phenomenon he was likely to dwell on. What strikes me most, in both of his notes, is the evocation of an inner counsel, wise and benevolent, only to be followed by this other, more critical commentator.

I hear it now in my own head: *OK OK—enough already!*

Even an overcast day can be *très belle* in Paris when you get to walk around with a newly twenty-one-year-old daughter. My father had been in London the night Molly was born; after returning home he'd written a letter to my husband.

30 January 1988

Dear Jeremy,

On the airplane the morning after Molly was born, I read this in Tom Wolfe's new book:

> And in that moment Sherman made the terrible discovery that men make about their fathers sooner or later. For the first time he realized that the man before him was not an aging father but a boy, a boy much like himself, a boy who grew up and had a child of his own, and as best he could, out of a sense of duty, and perhaps, love, adopted a role called Being a Father, so that his child would have something mythical, and infinitely important: A Protector, who would keep a lid on all the chaotic and catastrophic possibilities of life.[7]

All fathers feel this way, I'm sure: we're still boys, but the children don't realize it, and that may be the beauty of it. Grandfathers, of course, are just what they seem to be.

Much Love,

Bob

Recently, Jeremy came across that letter again. He really hadn't understood what it meant at first, he told me, because he hadn't been a father long enough. I asked what it means to him now.

"I see it as a kind of premonition of what we each would become," he said. "I had no idea what kind of father I would be. And your father couldn't have known what kind of grandfather he would be, though he probably sensed it would be a less complicated role."

Boys, girls, mothers, fathers, grandmothers, and grandfathers; it's like looking into the wrong end of a telescope through time and seeing, to paraphrase William Wordsworth, *the child is parent of the adult*.[8] Regardless of gender, the years pass both fast *and* slow as we carry with us who we are, who we've been, and who we are becoming. The day itself passes both fast and slow as Molly and I wander for hours in and out of the small shops of Le Marais. We amble down stone-paved streets, passing in and out of neighborhood "pocket parks," and finally, with the afternoon sky turning pink, limp back to my brother John's place for dinner.

After food and rest, John walks Molly and me to the Metro stop at the Arc de Triomphe. Before descending the stairs to head back to our hotel, we walk over to the eternal flame at the Tomb of the Unknown Soldier. Standing here, at the heart of *L'Etoile*—where a dozen Paris avenues converge in the shape of a twelve-pointed star—I've never felt so much at the center of everything. Bright lights and fast-moving cars fan out in twelve directions as we stand at the hub, the heart of a city that's lit up and in motion.

That night I wake with my whole body abuzz with sensation. A place that I imagine as the column of my own esophagus lights up with energy. Wide awake, I think of my father and the unknown road he is traveling. The inner hum coheres into an image and the twelve grandchildren appear. First, his namesake, Bobby, followed one by one by the rest of them. A circle forms, the grandchildren connecting to one another through interweaving pathways of light, and in the center, their beloved grandfather. The flame from the Arc de Triomphe appears as a warm steady glow. I see my father in the glowing heart of the circle along with everything he's going through: the tumor, the light, fear and not knowing, spaciousness and hope. The twelve streets that ray out in twelve directions become the twelve grandchildren.

In this inner vision, as the twelve spokes continue streaming out and beyond, my three brothers join me in forming four equidistant points around the center where my mother now joins my father. I sense how each of the four of us holds a distinct place in relation to our parents, yet together we form a coherent shape and share a common care and focus. The geometry of family relationships arises as image, sense, and feeling. Then it all falls away into the dark of night.

Waking the next day, I'm aware of a residual hum as I muse upon numbers making shapes, points on a circle of cousins, and the mystery of twelve. A transformative number, *twelve:* the number of parts that make a whole—months in a year, numbers on the clock, eggs in a dozen, inches in a foot, signs of the zodiac. How is this process we're entering with my father about collective transformation? It's not just his journey. How will the journey change us all?

Landing in Rome, we learn that Molly's huge suitcase never made it from Paris, whether due to size, the airport workers' strike, or simply bad luck. Twice a day we return to the hotel and make calls about the missing bag. The rest of our days are spent walking. Somewhere on the streets of Roma, an earring from a favorite pair of mine falls off. It is strange and unsettling to know so little Italian, to feel loss and confusion when surrounded by an unfamiliar language.

We spend an afternoon in Campo de' Fiori, *Field of Flowers,* watching the dismantling of the stalls, the passage from day to evening—market by day, restaurants and bars by night. The vendors move quickly, packing up their unsold crates of fruits and vegetables, baskets of flowers, ceramics, kitchen gadgets, T-shirts, and souvenirs. People are yelling over the clanging of the metal frames that are being folded and stacked in piles. I feel a dark heaviness in this busy square, a clutter and chaos that reflects my inner fears about my father. I'm both drawn to the tumult and want to run from it. But I'm also here as a pilgrim.

In the middle of this public square stands the towering, cape-domed figure of Giordano Bruno, who, over 500 years ago, was found guilty by the forces of the Inquisition for envisioning and promoting the radical idea that the earth circles the sun and for believing in an infinite universe. His statue marks the place where he was burned to death in 1600. I first heard Bruno's name in the early 1980s as an audience member watching a mesmerizing dance called PA RT,[9] performed to the first and last sections of what would become Robert Ashley's spoken opera, *Perfect Lives*.[10] The final act begins:

> She makes a double life.
> She makes two from one and one.
> She makes a perfect system every day.
> She makes it work.

Anyone who has heard Robert Ashley speak these words while dancers Lisa Nelson—with a painted-on mustache and Punjabi-style pants—and Steve Paxton—in James Joycean sunglasses, lean white pants, and a black muscle T-shirt—move together and separately in, with, and between the hypnotic riddle of the music, cannot ever read these words without the full sensorium of the experience reigniting every line.

After the hermetic welcoming of the number two, and subsequent discursions on the mystery and specificity of numbers, we hear Ashley say:

> Uncertainties are wrong.
> In this scene there is one shot.
> Giordano Bruno comes to mind, whoever he is.

Over the years since that performance, this is exactly how Giordano Bruno has appeared in my mind. Without knowing exactly who he was, I found him taking up occasional residence in my thoughts, a representative of a long line of rebel seekers of esoteric knowledge. The absence of detail enhanced the mystery already made atmospheric and transmissible by Nelson, Paxton, and Ashley.

I started reading the latest biography of Bruno on the flight from Paris. Now I'm eager to get back to it. After we leave Campo de' Fiori, Molly goes to meet some friends, and I head back to our hotel room. Not completely ready to leave the lively street below, I open a window and lean out into the cool evening air. Car horns and the lilting voices of passersby rise into the room as I turn to settle in and learn more about the nomadic Dominican monk.

The biographer, Ingrid D. Rowland, depicts Bruno as a philosopher-scholar who is testing, in his own mind, the implications of Copernicus's heliocentric theory. I'm fascinated by his thoughts about time, quoted from one of his last published books:

> Past time or present, whichever you happen to choose, or the future: All are a single present, before God an unending oneness.[11]

Bruno performs such a neat trick here, placing *you* in the middle of time's infinite span of unending oneness. *You*, the one who chooses, in a seemingly happenstance way, to be in a point of time—past, present, future—before God.

Can we choose time? Or is time conditioned? We may not do it consciously, but we are always choosing time. Reflecting on the past, imagining the future, and being in the present moment—each of these are perspectives of time, dependent upon the state of mind of the "viewer." What if we could see this? See it like the Renaissance architect and painter, Filippo Brunelleschi saw space as point of view. Giordano Bruno is inviting us to practice *seeing through time*, to see and experience ourselves living more consciously within the phenomenon of time.

Since my father's illness, when I am with him, the words "stay present" are like an amulet in my pocket. Pay attention to detail, the words say—his level of fatigue or discomfort, the mood in the room, a report from a doctor. The quality of this attention calls for a soft vigilance and acquiescence to whatever is happening without trying to interpret or change the situation. When I attend in this way, I sometimes experience an inner feeling of spaciousness, opening like the gates of a dam. My perception of time becomes space that flows and my father and I are together in the same stream of experience—"a single present."

Bruno continues:

> God chooses what he wants, he grants it, he knows it, creates it... Nothing can ever be done without his willing its doing, For he is fate itself; he is the divine will in person.[12]

Before I can get to the question that's forming in my mind, I have to erase any image of God that imposes itself each time I read the words *he* and *his*. It's an imperfect effort but at least it refocuses my attention on the *mystery* of divine will. However hard I try to overlook them, the pronouns evoke a figurative God persona, a form far too limited to warrant the words, "for he is fate itself."

I try to imagine this "choosing" by a God beyond imagination. Divine choice, so seemingly different, so vastly more primal and absolutely aloof from human choice. What is a choosing that is granting, knowing, and creating all wrapped in one? And then the question that has been slowly forming arrives: *What is the relationship between will and time?*

In Bruno's description of God's will, there is no temporal gap between the act of creation and the consciousness of what is being created. Human will in relation to human consciousness is rife with gaps in time.

A simple case in point: the missing suitcase. Packed in New England, repacked in Paris, intended to meet us in Rome, the bag is somewhere, we hope still in transit. Molly is convinced it will never get here. The Italian director of her program tells her not to worry since most lost bags eventually show up.

Bruno's words, his shadowed presence in Campo de' Fiori, and now the sounds of traffic and voices in the night awaken in me a feeling of alertness, a sense of continuity and meaning. What if everything from the most exalted to the most mundane moments of our earthly lives participates in this infinite and evolving universe in a purposeful way? Here we are, human beings in the twenty-first century, learning to be aware of our own attention, where it is focused, when it wanders, and how conscious we can be to what is present *now*. Anticipating relativity by 400 years, Bruno writes: "We may say that the sun which remains eternally one and identical, appears with a different face according to different observers."[13]

Over eight billion people under one sun; our family saga is just one among the myriad of many. I try to fathom how the different experiences and perspectives—my own, and those of my father, mother, husband, daughters, son, brothers, nieces, nephews, medical personnel, friends, encountered strangers—are all transpiring and co-existing. This nexus of activity around my father's illness is only one tiny constellation linking to a universe of other tales and constellations of individuals navigating their own life-changing loves and losses. A continuous unfolding.

OK OK
Time to call it a night.

The next day, after a trip to the department store for a few items of essential clothing, Molly joins the other students at the convent that will be their home for the next four months. (Her suitcase will arrive three weeks later.) After we say good-bye, I walk through the residential neighborhood of Aventino and over to the Palatine Hill and the Roman Forum. The ancient stone structures are impressive, but the most powerful places are the ones where plants and trees are growing. Grass and moss emerge between the cracked pathways. Wild, sprawling bushes climb the temple ruins. The walls may crumble, but the elemental world still comes looking for us.

Somewhere in here, like a golden thread of honey, runs *la vita*, life. Within my troubling story, begun with the news of my father's cancer, lives the sweetness of life continuing. Perhaps it's the joy of being with Molly, her adult life spreading before her. Or perhaps it's the time on my own, listening to my thoughts and the night sounds of a remarkable city. Following a meandering path with no set destination. The keen edge of fear feels like a blunt instrument compared to this, the delicacy and wakeful sharpness of being alive within the vastness of the unknown.

Touch the page
...your hands
your cheek...
touch the boundary
of your own simple, separate self
no other like you
ever seen
in the universe

THREE

Descending through layers of gauzy gray, the plane prepares to land in Boston. I return my seat to its upright position as multiple mental to-do lists vie for my attention. And just like that, I'm back in my regular life. The availability of time to muse about the meaning of time becomes, once again, an elusive luxury.

But I can't stop thinking about time. Even though I don't know what the future holds, it appears, in retrospect, already embedded in what is and what was. Since I learned of my father's cancer, memories from the past have gained new significance. The future was moving toward us. It only needed a diagnosis.

Last summer, before we knew what we know now, my parents came to Rhode Island for a visit. They wanted to spend a night in Newport, and they encouraged Jeremy and me to spend the afternoon with them seeing the sights and strolling along the Cliff Walk. When we arrive at their hotel room, we notice that my father is using a cane because of recurring back pain and that my mother is stretched out on the bed, icing her foot after jamming her heel on a poorly lit step. She is also in pain but insists, after a short rest, that she can keep going. Jeremy and I head off to find a drugstore to get my mother her own cane.

It is a beautiful, cloudless day. There is no way we're going to waste it lying around a hotel room. *Cliff Walk, here we come!* It is not until we are on the stone path looking down at the waves below, that the incongruity hits me. My ever-ready-to-engage-with-the-world parents are both hobbling along with canes. In that instant of recognition, the ground beneath me drops away, a swoon of vertigo and an ominous feeling that something is changing. I step to my right, closer to the grassy bank, a little farther from the cliff's edge.

My father's back pain, of course, turned out to be symptomatic of his cancer. And after the Newport incident, my mother continued to have difficulty walking. Now, while waiting for my suitcase at the baggage carousel back in Logan Airport, I call my parents. My father, who started chemo treatment while I was away, sounds upbeat. He says he's feeling tired but, so far, pretty good. My mother tells me she's scheduled foot surgery in a week.

"Can you come stay with us for a few days after my operation?" she asks.

I arrive in Stamford on a cold, damp February day. Fat snowflakes are falling as I drive up to the front curb of the outpatient clinic. Waiting in a wheelchair, my mother sits just inside the door, her lower leg in a cast. As I help her into the car, the accompanying nurse tells me it will be almost a week before my mother will be able to use crutches. She'll need to rest until then.

"You just be the queen and let everyone take care of you," she tells my mother.

Before we can pull out of the parking lot, my mother turns to me and says, "Because I had the operation now, I'll be in better shape to support your father." Even being bedridden is a mission for my mother.

Each night, she and I sleep head-to-head on the L-shaped couch in the first-floor room my parents call "the library," even though it's mostly used to watch television. By day, the room becomes command central. By night it turns into a summer camp scene as my mother and I lie there, talking past midnight like chatty cabinmates. In the morning when we wake, my father is already in the kitchen making breakfast for us all, classical music filling the air. By evening, the music will have changed, often to one of his old favorites, Nina Simone or John Lewis, or his latest discovery, the deep gravelly voice of Tom Waits.

I'm awed by my parents' energy and ability to surge forward. My father, as he always has, rises early. He's gathered piles of books he's long wanted to read and is steadily making his way through the volumes. He goes to the gym every other day and makes a special tea each morning as recommended by a friend who is thriving after being told his cancer was incurable. I don't know if my father actually drinks the slightly foul-smelling brew through the day, but he good-naturedly carries a thermos of it with him wherever he goes.

During the week with my parents, I tell them about Mariposa, a fledgling education initiative. A small group of us—educators and community members—have been planning and envisioning a center focused on the importance of the first seven years in providing the essential foundation for a child's whole life. We intend for it to be a place that values beauty, nature, health, and family, as well as artistic and contemplative practices. A place where teachers will nurture and protect each child's emerging sense of self. A place accessible to any child and welcoming to all families. A couple of Waldorf early childhood teachers have joined us to help with our initial pilot programs including, a few months ago, a test-run of our parent-toddler program.

I had volunteered to help one of the teachers get everything set up in the music classroom made available to us by a charter school in Providence. The transformation of the space is well underway by the time I arrive. A gentle, welcoming mood is created by a few strategically placed pastel cloths draped over a row of computers and filing cabinets, a peach-colored tablecloth with a vase of flowers and a central rug cleared of the extra chairs and plastic bins.

There are baskets of wooden toys and blocks on the rug, a few cloth dolls in a wooden cradle. Everything is simple, calm, beautiful. I wonder what the parents will make of it. For a parent struggling to find a job or working double-shifts, would it seem too precious? Would it be too incongruous in relation to what is so often called, "the real world"? My task on this day is to set aside such questions, and simply observe.

One mother and her two daughters arrive early. The teacher invites the mom to help fold the yellow child-size cloth napkins that will go on the table. The older daughter, a four-year-old, carries her nine-month-old sister to the middle of the rug, letting her slide out of her arms before turning to one of the baskets and emptying the contents onto the rug. She looks around the room and quickly discovers a plastic bin overflowing with naked Barbies and doll clothes that I had hidden under a desk. Carrying the bin to the rug, she empties it as well, then stands back while the younger sister reaches and rolls amidst the stew of doll paraphernalia.

The older sister pulls the younger one off the pile of doll clothes, ripping a miniature ball-gown from the baby's mouth and dragging her across the room to the corner. I feel my stomach tense and I reflexively lean forward to rescue the younger one, wanting to do something to prevent potential mayhem. I glance over at the teacher and the mother, who both sit calmly chatting, with the children in their line of vision. So I too sit back, soften my gaze and, as discretely as possible, "watch" the two sisters tumble together on the edge of roughness. The older one gives a soft slap to the head of the younger one, then looks to her mother, who is talking with the teacher. After getting no response from her mother, the big sister leans sideways, falling slowly to the ground. She curls herself into a mound-like shape and lets the younger one climb on top of her. For a few minutes they both lie completely still, resting.

Later that day, when I remember the clutched feeling in my stomach, I realize that the scene has stirred memories abiding deep in my nervous system, of being the oldest and only sister of three rambunctious brothers. Remembering more details from my observations, I am again moved by the power of mood and presence that the teacher offered. The morning unfolded with purpose and spaciousness. Other families arrived. The children played, the mothers (that day there were no fathers) talked quietly with the teacher, with each other, and watched the children from the edges of the rug. The teacher guided everyone through circle games, songs were sung, and then we gathered at the table for a snack of apples, cheese, and fresh-baked pumpkin bread.

Before the food was passed, the teacher led us in a blessing of gratitude for the food, for the sun, rain, and earth. I noticed the mom who came early holding her nine-month-old and wiping a few tears from her own eyes. As she was leaving, she told us that the morning itself had been a blessing, a kindness she would take home with her.

I know how hard it is to do what this gifted teacher did. It looks so simple. When my own children were younger, I tried to cultivate this quality of mood at home, covering the TV with a soft-colored silk, setting up a story table with wooden figures, and seasonal objects from nature, using minimal plastic. Creating a calm mood through décor is the easy part. Developing it as an inner strength and way of seeing, feeling, and being is much more difficult. Human life tests our capacity for equanimity every single day.

I tell my father about the parent-toddler program and our dream of creating a center for transformative early childhood teaching and learning. He asks good questions about the plans and wants to understand what makes Mariposa "transformative." The word sounds both obscure and commonplace as a measure of profound and lasting change. What my father is really asking is: How does it happen? What are the conditions?

"It begins with the space," I tell him. "First, we prepare the room where we meet the families." Then I realize that this is all I really know right now. Except that it also begins with who is in the room—both who shows up and who is there to welcome them.

Once a week, a group of us arrive at the same charter school where we did the pilot program. We unpack our cars loaded with soft dolls and wooden toys, play-stands and pastel-colored cloths, along with a few baskets of shells, stones, and blocks made from fallen branches, cut and sanded smooth—open-ended materials from nature to inspire the children's imaginative play. The austere music classroom on loan to us becomes a warm, inviting place. Then, as the teacher greets parents and toddler siblings of some of the current charter school children, her assistant is cooking oatmeal in the cafeteria kitchen, its comforting smell reminding me that a warm meal can be more important to learning than the latest tech device.

I also tell my father about an upcoming event at my teaching studio that I hope will raise some funds for Mariposa. I've invited Arthur Zajonc, a physicist, educator, and long-time teacher of meditation in the tradition of anthroposophy, to be our featured speaker and share his insights on the importance of contemplative approaches to teaching and learning.[14] I first heard Arthur speak on this subject while studying with him in an innovative graduate program designed to integrate academic research, contemplative inquiry, and practice in the arts. His deep understanding of the role that contemplative practices can play in scientific and research-based inquiry have inspired many, and his talks are always a rousing blend of the aspirational and the practical.

After a long pause, as my father looks out the window taking in what I've said, he turns to me and asks, "But what does Arthur's work in higher education have to do with children playing and eating oatmeal?"

And so begins a conversation about the child's state of wonder and curiosity being the root of what can blossom into artistic *and* scientific inquiry. We talk about the ways our formative experiences and early learning prepare the cognitive foundation for what will, in time, develop into the capacity for analytic thinking.

"I never thought about imagination being the basis for our intellect," says my father. "But it makes sense."

I ask if he remembers moments of wonder from his childhood.

He tells me about being a young boy, spending summers on the Indiana dunes of Lake Michigan. And the canoe trips, from the time he was twelve, on the lakes of northern Ontario.

"It was the water and the trees, the smell of sap and pine needles, the campfires at night, the sounds of birds, and the sense that we were visitors in a world that belonged to the animals." I notice that as he speaks he becomes very still.

"I remember how big the sky looked from the center of the lake," he continues, "and how small I sometimes felt, sitting in my canoe. And you never knew what the weather would do next."

"In some way," he says, "those early experiences in nature have guided my life. Even now, I always get my best ideas when I'm on the water in my kayak."

I follow his gaze out the window. The high tide winter water of Long Island Sound looks dark and unwelcoming. "If it wasn't so cold," says my father, "I would be out there right now."

A few weeks later, a group of Mariposa supporters show up to hear Arthur's talk. I always appreciate how far beyond utilitarian applications he brings us: encouraging us to approach our daily meditations with reverence, humility, and wonder; reminding us that the discipline of practice, after all, is grounded in an ethos of service and gratitude. Arthur describes contemplative inquiry as a process of "cognitive breathing." He explains that, instead of air, we breathe light through two distinct modes of attention. To experience this, he tells us, we can begin by focusing our attention on sensory phenomena: an object, an image, a word, or a phrase. After a few minutes of building up a picture and contemplating the chosen content, we let it go, our attention still present but now with wide-open awareness.

With a finger in the air, Arthur draws a horizontal figure eight, calling it a *lemniscate*, the mathematical symbol for infinity. He describes how first we can attend to the object of inquiry in the left side of the lemniscate. Then, when we let the focus of attention go, we are in the emptiness of the right-hand side where paradoxically even the figure eight, as an image, disappears. Being with the emptiness opens us to the possibility of an insight arising. Arthur suggests it comes as grace, and he shares a quote from Simone Weil:

> Grace fills empty spaces, but it can only enter where there is a void to receive it, and it is grace itself which makes this void.[15]

Arthur then invites us to experience contemplative inquiry for ourselves, suggesting we choose an image or phrase that has meaning for us. The memory from the Arc de Triomphe and the vision of my father at the shining center of a circle of grandchildren immediately comes to my mind. Into the left side of the lemniscate, I picture each of the cousins around my father at the center. When the circle is complete it begins to move, at first turning upright like a Ferris wheel before rotating to the horizontal plane like a plate. Then the whole image, now a three-dimensional transparent globe, slowly spins.

I see my mother joining my father at the center, the grandchildren encircling their Mermer and Boppa, as they affectionately call them. My brothers and I, along with our spouses, take our places, hovering in four spots around the outer perimeter. The image is more subdued than when I first experienced it that night in France. As my attention focuses on my parents, the globe is gone, replaced by memories: the stories of how they met as teenagers, how they fell in love, how they started their life together.

Now it's time to intentionally let go of the image, thoughts, and stories. *Empty mind, but not still mind.* A wave-like pulse is here. The pulse becomes a kind of undulating flow from front to back, back to front. And then a thought: *nothing is happening,* followed by a feeling of impatience: *nothing is going to happen.* And then a fuzzy image, a curled-up form lying on the ground that I recognize as me, tired and small. Disappointment. That's not the insight I wanted.

Release the want... Wait...not knowing.

It's when I'm not looking that something comes—the sense of a path before me. I recognize it as my path, my life unfolding. Other paths appear, other people's lives. My path is intersecting, paralleling, veering away from, and meeting other paths. I experience a web of activity, pulsing with movement and light.

A bell rings to end the meditation. Arthur suggests we close with gratitude for our experience, whatever it is. My heart is full. I look around the room, still feeling the pulsing web, seeing the faces of the others, each with their own invisible experience, their own path and life.

This glimpse of wholeness and interconnectedness is affirming and yet, within a day, I am once again that small, tired, uncertain self. How easily I slip back into the familiar place of separation. The voice of doubt rises: *Will any of this help me help my father?* I remind myself: *This is why it is a practice.* I remember reading a quote from Art Hodes, another of my father's jazz heroes: "My doctor once told me, 'I haven't arrived, I practice medicine.' Me too," writes Hodes, "I haven't arrived. Just making the trip daily."[16]

Making the trip, day by day by day.

It was in 1947 at a sanatorium for tuberculosis that my father listened to his first jazz record. When pondering my father's ease with time, I sometimes reflect on this as a period in his life when I imagine he learned, by necessity, to live day by day. He was fifteen when a misdiagnosis of TB led to his spending a good part of his sophomore year of high school, away from home, living on a ward with a lively group of sickly men who taught my father how to play poker. They welcomed him into their late-night games, sharing their cigarettes and contraband liquor with him. His parents brought him a record player and when she visited, his mother often brought one or two jazz records, which they would listen to together. Most days he was frequently alone resting or reading, often outside in the open air.

Half a year went by before it was determined that my father did not have tuberculosis after all and he was released from the Naperville Sanatorium. Along with a solid beginning jazz collection, he brought home an addiction to cigarettes, an appetite for booze, and an extra twenty-plus pounds due to the lack of exercise and the copious daily servings of ice cream, considered at that time part of the cure.

One miracle of this story is that in the midst of such prolonged exposure to others who actually had tuberculosis, my father did not contract the disease. But the underside of the miracle is that this forced convalescence happened—it was an event in his life that no doubt shaped my father, leaving a significant imprint upon his body and psyche. Yet it was something he rarely spoke of and when he did, it would be a sentence or two, mostly focused on the smoking, the gambling, the jazz, and the weight he gained. The bare bones of a story. Nothing about his inner life or how that year changed him.

Maybe this is the kind of experience that resists becoming a story. The kind of experience that lives on within a body as the cellular memory of courageous endurance. A silent impulse that if it could speak would say: *Keep going. Stay with it, even though it's hard and you don't know why this is happening… follow it, let it take you where it is going.* And maybe that subterranean, pre-audible voice is the dawning of a subtle, guiding presence within.

While the wide world
spins
the inner realm beckons
beyond the veiling
darkness
of
your eyes
closing

FOUR

Even before emerging full blown in green, pink, and yellow, spring is stirring underground. When my children Molly, Sam, and Julia were young, every March we had a ritual on the equinox. We would take fresh eggs, hold them carefully upright on the floor, sensing for the right moment to let go. A hush of wonder accompanied the minute or two we could all be still enough for the eggs to stand balanced on their own. Now, as I walk to my studio on this gray, damp day, this is the active stillness I imagine beneath my feet, a gathering of forces—gravity, light, the elements—rousing every seed, inviting life to root and rise.

The front door of the old Victorian house is big and heavy, requiring sensitive turning of both key and doorknob. The smaller door at the top of three flights of stairs leads to the attic room where I teach the Discipline of Authentic Movement. Today I'm taking time before my students arrive to tend to myself with a movement practice. Fitting the trips to Stamford into my already busy life leaves me grateful but blurry—rushed at every turn and out of balance. Where am I?

From the upstairs entry, I open another door and step into an open space unburdened by purpose or the weight of furniture, family photos, unread magazines, or even carpeting. The plain undemanding presence of an empty room, a place where a musing mind can meet the light streaming through the window. This is where unknowing lives. Now that I'm here, I feel welcomed, like coming home at the end of the day to a house that has waited patiently for my return.

Stepping into the space, I pause and wait for an impulse to move. At first, there is nothing but standing in place. But then I become aware of my head turning, tilting back, as if listening into the wind, turning toward something—I don't know what. I notice a feeling of wanting

35

to be simple, unadorned, and empty, like the room. And a sense that something palpable and true will meet me here.

Since 1990, I have studied and practiced the Discipline of Authentic Movement. Often, when someone hears this for the first time, they ask how or when a movement could ever be inauthentic. I usually reply, "It can't." But from a contemplative perspective, the word *authentic* refers to the inner discovery of being present within your embodied experience. The authentic aspect of movement is not about what's right or perfect in some externally measured or definitive way, it's about what's inwardly true for you.

My first intentional foray into the terrain of inner experience happened in my early twenties when I was a dancer recovering from a difficult knee surgery. For two months, through an icy winter, I was confined indoors, constrained by a full-length leg cast, feeling betrayed by my body at the very time I thought I had found my calling in dance. It was a period of frustration, questioning, and sometimes despair. After a year of painful rehabilitation, a series of sessions with a somatic practitioner offered the deeply satisfying discovery that body and mind can converse for mutual benefit.

Opportunities for further exploration appeared after I began dancing again. During my recovery from surgery, I developed unconscious habits, like the subtle way my left leg would protect the right by bearing more weight. I was suffering from pain caused by misalignment, reinforced by daily acts of compensation. My physical therapist suggested I see Eva Karczag, a teacher of the Alexander Technique, who helped her through similar challenges after an injury.

It was with Eva that I discovered that joints are more than bony structures. It's the space between bones that makes movement possible; the tension we carry constricts space, thus inhibiting motion. By becoming conscious of the source of tension, a different choice of action becomes possible. It was a revelation for me to experience the feeling-sense of my body as simultaneously spacious and substantive. How flat my sense of self and the world had been. Here was a whole new way of knowing and a far more dimensional way of being. I was able to experience what *up* and *above* are by feeling the ground, a sense of *down* and *beneath,* under my feet. I learned to be more open and present to what's in *front* of me by being more aware of the fullness of my *back*. This embodied way of knowing was different from my usual way of thinking about whatever I was doing.

After experiencing the Alexander Technique as a direct transmission of expansion and ease through Eva's voice, touch, and presence, I told her I wanted to learn how to teach this method. That's when Eva introduced me to Aileen Crow. Over the next five years, Aileen became an extraordinary guide, training me as a teacher while fearlessly, lovingly, helping me welcome parts of myself that emerged through our study and exploration of the Alexander principles, movement patterns, and hands-on inquiry. With Aileen all of this was supplemented by a guided tour into the realm of the psyche—from her I learned that even parts of us that live in the shadows of consciousness play active roles in our lives. Engaging these hidden parts of my personal history was both scary and liberating.

Working with Aileen, I discovered a sense that being born had not been easy for me. Embodied awareness experiences opened an inquiry into what my body remembers from my own birth. By following spontaneously emerging movement, I started to recognize particular patterns. My head would tuck up against my upper arm and shoulder, unable to move. Other times, my head would push against the floor in a rocking motion that seemed to have no end. Feeling stuck was a familiar and disconcerting state. Eventually I learned to tolerate the fear and discomfort, realizing over time that if I stayed with the feeling and didn't try to change it, I would feel a sense of being released from the pattern, followed by a drifting sense of drowsiness.

When I asked my mother what she remembered about my birth, she told me it had been challenging. She wanted to give birth naturally, a relatively uncommon desire in the late 1950s, and especially brave considering that barely a year earlier she had delivered a full-term stillborn baby boy. The conventional wisdom was to move on quickly from such a loss—*don't think about it, don't let your feelings get you down.* It was a different era when birth, illness, and death were generally considered taboo subjects.

I was the baby born following this unspoken loss and unfelt grief. Because I was stuck, my head pressing and hitting against my mother's pelvic bone, she was given anesthesia and I was pulled out with forceps. Surviving a difficult birth, I was the baby who lived, welcomed into the world with relief and gladness.

The feeling of being stuck was later echoed in aspects of my knee injury. In the weeks before surgery, my orthopedic doctor had me wear a brace he called "the immobilizer." Even now, the feeling is here as I think about my birth, about my knee, and even about my father's illness. My body responds to each of these with the same inner bracing—a contraction behind my solar plexus, something pressing out against something pressing in. The sensate feeling is of being both frozen and suspended; the emotion is distress and helplessness, the feeling of not being able to do anything about what is happening.

Many years of somatic study, meditation, and self-inquiry have created rich opportunities to learn from these early patterns and feelings. Immobility became the portal to a new inquiry. Finding my way through the feeling of being stuck meant listening to my body, tolerating not knowing, respecting the unfolding of experience, and meeting whatever was ready to emerge as more conscious awareness.

After I finished training with Aileen, my husband Jeremy and I moved with our eighteen-month-old daughter Molly to Rhode Island. In the process of looking for colleagues and establishing my own Alexander Technique teaching practice, I was invited to a film showing about Authentic Movement and the work of Janet Adler. I was intrigued and joined a group led by Diana Levy, a local teacher who had studied with Janet.

Some of Janet Adler's approach was familiar from my work with Aileen. Permission to follow an inner impulse without knowing where it would go was beyond familiar; it felt essential to the person I was becoming as a teacher and young mother. What was new was the quality of Diana's understated, yet potent presence. She described her role as one of witness. She would sit on the periphery of the space while the rest of us closed our eyes, each mover waiting for or following an already active impulse to move, always free to follow the impulse or not. When we came together to speak after the movement time, Diana waited until each individual mover finished speaking before offering that mover her spare, but affirming, verbal witnessing.

"The mover is the expert of her or his own experience," Diana said, telling us how Janet had adopted this phrase from one of *her* teachers, John Weir, a master psychologist. What a radical and yet completely sensible perspective: Not only is the phenomenon of my own inner experience worth paying attention to, no one else can know it better than I can! The implication is that we are each the expert of our own experience. As a group we were learning a whole new premise for relationship with self and with others: relationship rooted in self-authority. We were learning how to speak the language of our own embodied awareness, the language of movement, touch, and other sensations, of emotion, image, and memory. We were learning how to listen to others speak from *their* embodied experience.

After two years of meeting weekly, Diana encouraged our group members to travel to western Massachusetts for a weeklong retreat with Janet. Four of us signed up, and one October day we piled into a car for the three-hour drive to a rustic lodge in the hills of Hawley. The studio was in a semi-renovated old barn that had a warm wood floor and window views of bountiful vegetable gardens and an autumn-tinged hillside in the distance.

Midway through the week, I began to realize that a central question Janet brought to the work concerned the presence of the witness. This was a deep and sensitive inquiry into the lived experience of seeing and being seen. It was daunting and confusing to realize how much of my seeing was more reflective of me than of the mover, the one seen.

By the end of the week, I knew there was much more to learn. With Janet as my teacher, the practice itself—she calls it the Discipline of Authentic Movement—was a way to study, through lived experience, the presence or absence of consciousness in relation to myself, to others, and to my deepest questions about life and meaning. In Janet's work, the relationship between the one who moves and the one who witnesses sustains the evolution of embodied consciousness for both mover and witness. Janet describes this process as the development of the *inner witness*, a strengthening toward compassionate presence and a refining of the aspect of consciousness that observes experience.

The implications of this embodied and relational practice for other kinds of relationships, particularly between teacher and student, doctor and patient, or parent and child, continue to intrigue me. So much passes unnoticed in these critically important relationships. What if we could learn to consciously embody the quality of presence available in our roles as teacher, doctor, and parent? How would this enhance all we have to offer?

I place a small candle next to the blue vase of pussy willows on the round table in the entry room where I will soon welcome a new student. As I strike the match, in my mind's eye I see Janet's hands: one is holding a candle, the other lights the wick. I watch my own hands hold the candle, light the wick. The flame swells and then subsides, a soft glow. Gratitude. The gestures of our teachers—not just their words and tone of voice—their gestures live and move within us.

A few days later, I rearrange my life once again in order to spend a few days with my parents. Something is shifting in our relationship. I realize how much I have taken their care and watching of me for granted. Now it is my turn to watch them.

My mother is still healing from her foot surgery but can now drive herself to physical therapy sessions. My father has graduated from chemo to radiation but is losing weight by the week. One day, I go with him to the hospital for his treatment. On the way to an examining room, he introduces me to his new friend James, the radiation technician. While we wait for the nurse to arrive to take his vitals, he tells me how kind and careful James is. My father stands, lifting his shirt to show me the large red X on his belly, the target area for radiation, drawn as if by a finger dipped in earthy red pigment.

He looks down, watching his own finger slowly trace each line as it crosses the other. I watch too, as the traced X imprints itself in me, opening me to the vulnerability he is sharing, his soulful strength. His unguarded openness is what draws the nurses, the technicians, and the hospital custodians to him, his appreciation for the warmth of human exchange and the sense that we are all in this together.

The light is changing. Days start earlier, end later. We're well into spring, but it is impossible to tell by the temperature. Baseball has arrived, as it always does in New England, with a biting wind lacing even the sunniest days. Every year since my son Sam was five, baseball has been a defining feature of spring for our family. His first Little League team was the Hospital Trust Orioles, and so his favorite major league team for many years was the Baltimore Orioles. When he was quite a bit older, he explained that in his five-year-old mind, he believed his local team was the lowest rung of the whole Orioles organization. He and Cal Ripken, part of the same franchise, were teammates in a way.

My father always loved this story. I imagine it appealed to his sense of inclusiveness, his vision of a team or corporate body as a group where individuals support each other's development, where the role of elders in mentoring the younger ones would be taken seriously.

Now that Sam is a freshman playing baseball at Tufts University, my father is eager to get to a game. We make a plan for my daughter Julia and me to drive to Stamford, pick him up, and head north to Hartford to catch a doubleheader at Trinity College. Ironically, this is where Molly goes to school, only she's still in Rome on her semester abroad. As we walk from the car through the campus, we run into a couple of her friends, who join our slow stroll to the baseball field. Molly's boyfriend Max is there to meet us. I've brought a blanket for my father which we end up placing on the cold metal stands. Max goes to his dorm and returns with a few more blankets so my father is well-wrapped by the time the game begins.

It's all very exciting—Sam is playing second base and the team is playing well. The score is close for a few innings but ultimately, Tufts ends up losing the first game, 11–5. In the second game, Sam hits a double. When the next batter gets a hit, Sam slides home, scoring in a close play at the plate and emerging in a cloud of dust. My father cheering, leaps to his feet. Julia and I rearrange the blankets around him after he sits down again, but by the time the game ends, with a 2–1 loss, the temperature is dropping and there is no way to get my father warm enough. Once back at the car, we bundle him up again for the ride back to his house. While coughing much of the way home, he still manages to let us know "That was great!"

Playing sports was where I first became conscious of myself as a mover. The father-daughter games of rolling, catching, and chasing balls did not end with the arrival of my brothers. My father saw and encouraged my love of physical play. My mother recognized it, too, and took me to dance classes, but it was my father who would toss me in the air, race with me in the park, and later join in the football and hockey games with my brothers and me. Pure joy.

The summer I turned nine, my father invited me to take up tennis with him. He had never played much so we learned together, going to the public courts at Winston Churchill Park early Sunday mornings before the better players arrived who would be annoyed by our bad shots and our stray balls rolling into the middle of their games. Slowly, we began to improve, and one day I became aware of a man outside the court, watching us. In spite of my ineffectual lobs and backhands into the net, the man seemed to notice our camaraderie. He called out to my father: "She'll beat you yet!"

The attention was nice but what I remember most was my father's half-hearted smile, a mix of resignation, acceptance, and pride. Even then, I knew nothing would delight him more than for me to surpass his best efforts. Even now, I see that same type of joy whenever he watches one of his grandchildren competing or just playing around.

A week after the baseball road trip with my father, I'm back home trying to rush out the door to take Julia to soccer practice when I get a phone call from my mother. She is upset that my father is not going along with some of the healthy meals that she has put tremendous effort into planning and preparing. Sometimes, she tells me, he resists simple things like drinking water, which even the doctors encourage. Today, I am not much help. Between having one eye fixed on the clock so Julia won't be late, and not wanting to take sides but be supportive to both my parents, I find myself, with some distress, in the middle. I feel guilty that I have to hang up quickly.

Once out of the city, I drive past woods and scrubby-looking fields where not much is growing yet. I'm a poor traveling companion for my daughter, preoccupied with concerns for and about my parents. The sky darkens, raindrops fall, and the road begins to glisten as we near the practice field. This is Julia's favorite kind of soccer weather—the wetter, the better. As soon as we arrive, she hops out of the car and runs toward the huddle of girls already on the field. With a little less eagerness, I also step outside, open an umbrella, and wrap my coat more tightly around myself. I walk to an adjacent field and look for a place to unburden my worries. Leaning into the rain, gripping the umbrella, I make my way to a stone wall on the far side of the field. My hand reaches out, touching rock, feeling the rough skin of lichen through the wetness. And the tears come.

Crying brings some relief. The wet stone offers solace. As the rain falls harder, I retrace my steps. The ground sinks beneath my feet, my knees buckling a little with each step. I shake out the umbrella before getting back into the car. Through the swirling veil of water on the windshield, I watch Julia and her teammates run up and down the soccer field, drenched but not deterred by the downpour.

I open the book I've brought and read:

> At least since Freud, we know that unconscious forms seem equipped with a certain "intelligence" that helps them prevail. This trait gives them a kind of being, as if they were conscious or at least instinctive entities—even with a goal-directed slyness about them.[17]

The author, Georg Kühlewind, describes this "intelligence" or capacity to prevail as "expressed, open resistance to every attempt at improvement or healing." I stop reading and look up from the page. I find the idea that acts of resistance might be prompted by sly, instinctive beings utterly compelling. The rhythmic motion of the rain on the window takes me, holds me steady, as I think about how inner aspects of self might have agency and agendas of their own.

Staring out the window, I remember something I learned while studying with Aileen. She wanted us to understand the powerfully complex way that different parts of our psyche show up when we pay attention to our own behavior. She had us find a partner and choose a relatively minor problem in our lives to explore how we communicate with ourselves and what a problem might be trying to tell us.

I chose the problem of not remembering to floss my teeth. While processing this issue with my partner, I realized that one of the reasons for my resistance to remembering is that I don't like the way my dentist tells me I have to. By hearing this perspective of a part of me that doesn't like to be told what to do, I find myself in dialogue with this part. It has something to say. As I listen to the part that wants to have its own voice, I develop an awareness of other ways my desire to honestly express myself shows up in my life alongside my fear of what that might entail.

Aileen was a master of working in this way, exploring how our parts play out, with and against each other. With infinite curiosity and affection, she welcomed these wily internal impulses, gestures, and voices that drive our behavior, wait to be noticed, and are willing to be transformed. And, of course, nothing brings forth these subversive minions like our relationships with other people.

Sitting in the car, staring through the blur of rain, I find my thoughts turning again to my family. We are all invested in my father getting better, but my mother, who has everything to lose, has taken on the battle with especially fierce determination. Her prodigious research, experiments with raw foods, blood-type diets, healers, and daily walking meet my father's increasingly grumpy, but minimally confrontational resistance. My brothers and I have been watching our parents negotiate a common path forward in which he goes along with some things—like the pre-breakfast serving of sea cucumber jelly—and refuses others— like traveling to Colombia to see a psychic surgeon. All the while, he tries to preserve some degree of doing things his way.

Someone has scored a goal. Half the girls on the field run toward one another, arms raised high in the air. The rest of the girls walk or stand in place, waiting for the game to resume. I see the blurred inhabitants of the other cars, each of us in our own thoughts as we wait for practice to end. I return to my inner musings, wondering what the way forward will be.

Perhaps my father's resistance to my mother's entreaties and determination to heal him arises from a desire for his own autonomy, to find his own way between two allegiances—his wife and "the experts." On one side stands my mother, the love of his life, with her conviction that alternative and spiritually oriented approaches belong at the forefront of all attempts at healing. On the other side stands his faith in doctors, and his need to trust the power of western medicine to eradicate whatever ails him.

But who is the expert? Who is in charge? My father's primary care physician doesn't return any calls and has essentially disappeared. We spend a great deal of time trying to get answers, to get doctors to call back, to get them to coordinate with each other. With so many specialists, it has become complicated, especially since none of them seems to hold the whole picture. I think about my father: How *does* one orient oneself when faced with two distinct perspectives? Balancing family dynamics with the demands of the medical system, all while it's *your* life that's on the line. How does one find one's true way between the desperate longing to be well and the unknowable course of disease?

It feels like a clash between love and free will. What wouldn't the rest of us do to help him get well? Our determined efforts meet his noble and so very human drive for self-determination. No one wants to be told what to do. The more someone feels he or she has no choice, the more they look for ways to feel in control even if it takes the form of resistance. And for those of us who love my father, the cancer gives us no choice but to foist our good intentions upon him.

Soccer practice is ending, the rain has not let up. Wishing I had brought dry clothes for Julia, I step out of the car holding the umbrella open for her. Of course, as she reminds me, there's really no need—she's already soaking wet.

Memory stirs
in the dark
of body

you can choose
or not
to follow
it

FIVE

I haven't seen my father in over a month but here he is, stepping out of his house. I park my car in my parents' driveway and follow the front walk past the freshly blooming azaleas, up the stone steps, into my father's big, welcoming hug. Joy and shock converge as I feel his spine, his ribs—yet still, his strength. His embrace holds nothing back. I see he is running out of notches in his belt as he tells me that he's lost over forty pounds.

It's been a challenge to get enough calories through the food that's soft enough for my father to swallow. Mealtimes, always such a source of pleasure for him, are now daily reminders of how much his life has changed. My parents have been trying to address the weight loss with my father's oncologist, who alternates between being noncommittal and unavailable. But a plan has finally taken shape, and I'm here to accompany my parents to the hospital. It's time for a feeding tube to provide liquid calories to supplement his soft food diet. My father calls it his food pipe.

The next day, we get to the hospital by late morning only to learn that the procedure has been postponed until the end of the day. Not enough time to leave and come back, too much time to just sit browsing through magazines. We alternate short walks with long rests in the main waiting room until the hours pass and, at last, someone comes to escort my father to an interior waiting room. Two hours later, he is "in recovery."

While waiting for him to emerge, my mother and I try to get detailed instructions about the feeding tube, but anyone with the authority to answer our questions has already left for the day. We're told, however, that if he spends the night, one of the doctors and a nutritionist will come by his room between 8:00 and 8:30 a.m.

My mother and I return to the hospital by 7:30 the next morning. My father is awake and anxious to get going. A nurse shows us how to clean the bandages around the plastic plug that is now in my father's belly. A bag of pale white liquid hangs atop an IV pole, and we pay close attention as she connects the tube that runs from the bag to the plug. Breakfast slowly descends as my father watches with skepticism. He tells us how strange it is to be fed in such a passive way.

After the nurse leaves, we wait in anticipation of a nutritional plan and further technical guidance. I too feel overcome by a strange passivity. I look at my father in bed, propped up by extra pillows. He is staring at the snaking motion of the tube. My mother and I slump further into our plastic chairs, further into what has become a familiar lethargy of waiting with dimming expectations.

The team finally arrives just before noon. In less than a minute they dispense their message: "Five cans of Ensure spread throughout the day," before disappearing out the door. We're stunned by this medical minimalism but we dutifully help my father pack his belongings. Once we're all situated in the car, my mother drives us to the drugstore. While they wait in the car, I go in to buy a couple of cases of Ensure. Standing in the aisle for nutritional supplements, I check the ingredients on the back of the can. My heart sinks when I read the first five: water, sugar, corn syrup, corn maltodextrin, and milk protein concentrate, followed by a few vitamins and minerals. I can't believe this concoction can possibly help him.

Back at my parents' house, I help my mother set up an area of the kitchen for the feeding tube paraphernalia. I bookmark the URL of a medical webpage where they can find online assistance before hugging my parents and saying good-bye. I feel torn in a dozen ways. I wish I could stay to help my parents with my father's new meal regimen. Perhaps we can find another nutritional beverage that isn't full of sugar and corn syrup. At the same time, I can't wait to get back home to see Jeremy and Julia, and I have so much to do to catch up with my own life. Yes, I do feel torn.

On the car ride home, I call each of my brothers. We all agree the feeding tube is added insult to the pernicious injury of cancer. My father is resigned to a more restricted diet but we know he mourns for his sense of taste, now dulled by chemotherapy. This is a man who can describe in detail a meal he ate twenty years ago. Perhaps even more, he misses the culinary tasks of planning, shopping for ingredients, cooking, and serving meals to friends and family. It was just a month ago that my brother Jeff made a big stockpot of fish broth, fresh caught in Maine's Casco Bay. Carefully taping the top of the pot, he carried it on the train from Boston to Stamford. Special delivery: a healing elixir.

Over the days Jeff stayed with my parents, he created numerous meals from the broth, filling the freezer with containers of wonderful stews. My father was thrilled. It was a welcome opportunity to vicariously experience his favorite kind of cooking adventure. I can't help hoping that, for someone who loves food and flavor as much as my father, his sense of taste can live on in his vivid memory.

Back home at last, I open the front door and breathe in the garlicky aroma of Jeremy's herb-roasted chicken. He and Julia are waiting for me.

"Let's eat," I say.

My friend Gertrude Hughes,[18] a writer and educator, arrives the next day as our second guest speaker in what is now becoming a fundraising series for Mariposa. Gertrude gives an introductory talk and then leads us in discovering how poems and contemplative inquiry can work together to awaken creative and perceptive powers that lie dormant in our consciousness. I love how she describes poems as ways of preparing our hearts to think.

Gertrude reads aloud the poem, "Island," by Langston Hughes.[19] What a different kind of minimalism this is:

> Wave of sorrow,
> Do not drown me now:
> I see the island
> Still ahead somehow.
>
> I see the island
> And its sands are fair:
> Wave of sorrow,
> Take me there.

A heavy feeling catches me by surprise—my deep discouragement about my father's condition. The poem's simple words call to me in a soft, steady voice: *stay close*. They speak in syllable, plain and direct. The wave of sorrow is not symbol, not even image; it is experience. Gertrude invites us each to silently read the poem again. My feelings intensify. Risk of drowning feels imminent. The watery world of emotion is not my favorite place to be. I much prefer the solid ground of sensation or the airy realm of the thinking mind.

But here, the poem itself is a vessel. I let myself go under, feeling the swell of sadness. The *I* surfacing is the boat's captain: *I see the island*. The mast rights itself and new perception is here, hope is here. Hope imagines what may be. Hope has direction.

Will the sands be fair?

Unknowing is also here. I remember Janet's words, a phrase she learned from one of her teachers: "The only way out is in and through." And this the poem knows, too. Surrender to what is here, to what is true. Learning to trust feeling through feeling. *Wave of sorrow, take me there.*

Despite my initial misgivings after reading the ingredients on the back of the Ensure can, a few weeks later I'm relieved to hear that my father is gaining weight and feeling better. Then another month goes by without me being able to see him because of the happy news that Mariposa's grant application to participate in the Rhode Island Department of Education's Pre-Kindergarten Demonstration Project has been accepted. This is the beginning of public Pre-K in Rhode Island, and Mariposa is one of only a handful of programs statewide to be chosen. Eighteen children, picked by lottery, will be able to attend at no cost to the families. There is so much to do! The classroom and building site we planned to move into passes every inspection except the lead test so we need to find a new site, hire two teachers, purchase child-sized furniture, and complete a host of other tasks to get the classroom ready to welcome the children in September.

When I'm finally able to visit my parents again, my father is twenty pounds heavier, looking healthy again. In a stretch without chemo or radiation, he seems full of life. Glad to be outside after a long winter and cold spring, he invites me to join him on a kayak ride. We clean off the boats, drag them to the shore, and head off under a warm sun.

In a nearby marsh cove, we drift, staring up at a tree filled with egrets and gazing at the tall grasses along the shore. I lean back and let the kayak support me. I relax into a watery sense of time moving languidly forward, backward, in circles. The air feels thick with green foliage, with the soft rays of sun, with life and growth. Time floating, time dissolving, time absorbing into light.

An egret lets out a call, launches from the tree, glides through the air over our heads, then circles back to a higher branch. I rouse from my reverie and we slowly make our way through the cove back toward Long Island Sound. My father looks strong as he paddles beneath the clear blue sky. A steady roll of waves flows under our kayaks, rocking us gently from side to side. It's odd to feel waves on such a calm day, especially since there are no boats anywhere in sight.

I call out, "Where are the waves coming from?"

He calls back, "These are the waves of yesterday's wind."

We keep paddling, his words echoing—*the waves of yesterday's wind*—like it was a matter of fact. It may well be, but to me it sounds like poetry, with a little science and philosophy thrown in. Had he just made it up? It didn't matter. It was in my mind now along with the breeze and the quiet cries of gulls and the rhythm of my arms drawing figure eights with the paddle. I imagine the wind of a day ago somewhere far out on the sea setting these waves in motion, and I wonder: just what *is* traveling through water across distance and time?

Yesterday's wind and more. For my father, nature is alive with meaningful purpose. We are not here for exercise, though that's part of it. We are here to revel in the day.

The next morning, I drive my father into New York City for an endoscopic procedure to obtain a biopsy, something he morbidly enjoys calling his *autopsy*. Today his usual command of words is making room for a darker humor. Soon we will know the results of his months of chemo and radiation. Has the size of the cancer been reduced enough for surgery? If so, the procedure will be more arduous and daunting than his treatments thus far. As we slowly navigate the morning rush hour traffic, my focus on the road helps keep my fears at bay as I wonder what will happen next.

We've given ourselves plenty of time so even after parking the car on the street we've still arrived early enough to take a long, leisurely walk in the surrounding neighborhood, as if going to the hospital is just one of the interesting things we'll do today. I ask him, as we stroll, if he ever regretted leaving Canada.

"Oh no," he says, "there's so much that's happened for us all here."

As usual, his perspective includes everyone and everything. It's not just how *he's* done, but how each of us in the family has fared—all in all, okay. And it's not just the opportunities and good fortune, it's the challenges, disappointments, and setbacks: "there's so much that's happened."

He tells me about the day, at the beginning of his career, when he accidentally got a paycheck intended for someone else whose last name was one letter off from his, someone who had been working at the same company for almost twenty years. He was horrified to see that his senior colleague was making only slightly more than his own entry-level salary, a discovery that precipitated his search for a new job.

I knew from my mother that shortly after he became a senior director in the New York office of the company he worked at for decades, he learned how much more money upper echelon executives were making than those working immediately under them. Bothered by the inequity, he posted all the upper management salaries, including his own, so everyone could see the disparity. It was a way of pulling aside the veil, dispelling the mystique around compensation. He felt people ought to know where they stood. If they weren't making enough, maybe it was unfair. On the other hand, maybe they needed to work harder. Either way, he suggests, calls for honest self-reflection and a conscious course of action.

Ever the moralist, I add, "And maybe there's such a thing as making too much, especially if it's at the expense of others."

"Maybe, but what's most important," he says, "is that people should be compensated fairly." He didn't like that his company made up for less competitive wages by giving employees club memberships and larger travel allowances. However, his attempt to impact healthy discussion about more equitable salary structures failed and within a decade the gap began to grow vastly wider.

"It's obscene," he says, "that some CEOs now earn more in compensation than their company pays in corporate income tax."

My father was not averse to hierarchy, but he believed in fairness. He disliked rigidity and conformity. He had an inner ease that was made visible by his suit jackets with their soft, sloping shoulders and by his loafer-style shoes. From the time he was "rewarded" with his own office, he made sure it reflected his individual style—my mother's vibrantly colored abstract paintings on the walls, books he liked, family photos, and objects that had meaning for him. A six-inch-wide brass plaque on his desk, facing whomever he was meeting, especially intrigued me. Engraved on the plaque was a single sentence: "But here there are no cows."

Once, when I asked him what it meant, he told me to read Robert Frost's poem, "Mending Wall."[20] I'm confident this was the same non-explanatory answer my father gave colleagues and clients—inclined, like Frost in conversation with a rural neighbor, to a bit of "mischief":

> There where it is we do not need the wall:
> He is all pine and I am apple orchard.
> My apple trees will never get across
> And eat the cones under his pines, I tell him.
> He only says, "Good fences make good neighbors."
> Spring is the mischief in me, and I wonder
> If I could put a notion in his head:
> "Why do they make good neighbors? Isn't it
> Where there are cows? But here there are no cows.

Twice, elsewhere in the poem, Frost writes, "Something there is that doesn't love a wall." This *something* that doesn't love a wall is deeply rooted in my father. His perspective for solving any problem always begins with his classic line: "We're all on the same side." His professional attitude was: *if there's a wall, let's deal with it*—whether it was creating access to insurance for high-risk coverage, or removing impediments to women and people of color advancing to management positions.

My father's instinct for rapport had served him well in life. Words he spoke at the memorial for one of his closest workplace friends were equally true of himself: "For him, relationships were there to be cherished and tended in an atmosphere of unguarded trust." But I knew it had not always been easy for him. Throughout his career, my father was often typecast as "creative," and seen as someone who liked to stir up the status quo. I imagine his way of doing things, so idiosyncratic and intuitive, was not easily transferable to a corporate setting.

Walking back to the hospital, I ask him how he survived all those years in the insurance field, an industry that, to my outsider eyes, seems so conventional. But he doesn't take the bait.

"I love the insurance brokerage industry," he says. "Great people, challenging problems. But like everywhere, we need to do more to be welcoming, to attract and bring in more people with diverse backgrounds and perspectives."

By now we are a block away from the hospital and it's time to go in. Just before the entrance, my father stops walking. We stand facing each other in the middle of the sidewalk as he tells me one more story. An unexpected anecdote that explains how the doctors finally figured out that he didn't have tuberculosis during his year at the sanatorium.

"It was the mid-1940s," he tells me, "when drug trials were just beginning. I was chosen to be a guinea pig."

"Actually," he adds, "it was a couple of guinea pigs and a few mice who were chosen to participate in the trial experiments. I was the supplier of the pathogen. As it turned out, none of the animals contracted TB. So, it was a good day for all of us, but I was the one who got to go home."

With little time to reflect upon the solution of this particular mystery, I ask my father if he's ready to go in for the biopsy. "Sure," he answers. The stories end and we ride the elevator to the second floor in silence.

Later, as we drive back to Connecticut after the procedure, my father returns to one of our earlier conversations. His voice is soft and a bit hoarse.

"You know," he says, "it's a real opportunity to work with others to address what isn't working, to respond to what's new, to what's needed, but the biggest challenge, always, is fear of change. In my business that was always the obstacle."

After agreeing that fear of change is prevalent in just about every sphere of human endeavor, I ask if he's afraid of what the scope results might show.

"Of course," he says. "*And* we have every reason to be hopeful."

When I was growing up—feeling boundless in the natural world, small and cautious in social circles—I used the word "hopefully" a lot, as in "Hopefully I'll do alright on my exams," or "I'm going to meet my friend—hopefully—downtown." My father was not a fan of the phrase nor my frequent use of it. "It's not really a word," he would say.

Beyond any question of grammatical correctness, it seemed he was trying to tell me that using this word was a way of diminishing myself, a lazy and submissive way of being in relationship to life and the future. Of course, this annoyed me. Typical of my mild-mannered mode of rebellion, I continued to insert "hopefully" into most of my conversations until I was well out of college. Only after my own children were born did the word begin to disappear from my vocabulary, as I began to feel more securely centered in myself, less subject to a perpetual sense of my existence being dependent on luck.

While hope was a word my father used rarely, I have come to believe that sharing hope was part of our unspoken pact. *Hope* is an inner experience that draws strength from a source beyond ourselves; *hopefully* is wishful thinking. Hope is not passive when coupled with responsibility and commitment. Hope is the heart's orientation toward something unseen, a way of inwardly, yet actively, participating in the unfolding of our lives without any pretense of power to control the outcome. Hope is indeed our boat.

Somewhere along the river of days, we learn that the biopsy and scans show the cancer has been reduced in size. The tumor is still there but is now likely operable. We return to the hospital to meet with the oncologist and surgeon. This time my mother and brothers join us. After more than an hour in the waiting room, we convene in the surgeon's office, a long, narrow room with a big window that looks out over the city. Both doctors are already here. My parents sit close to them. The rest of us go to the chairs for family members, near the picture window.

The doctors seem so far away. One sits behind a desk. The other stands, arms crossed, in front of the desk, leaning into it and away from us. I feel disoriented, suddenly very small. We are in a Lilliput world where the doctors seem far above us, looking down from a strange, impersonal perspective. They are not particularly encouraging. My father will need to build up strength, the surgeon tells us, describing the scale of assault on his body. To remove the tumor, they will need to open him from his back and his front, up and down. They tell us this as if my father is not here in the room. They are impatient with our questions.

We leave deeply dismayed by their manner. Almost worse than their news was their indifference. There's little to say as we make our way to the elevator. Out on the street, one of us says, "Let's head to the park," so we turn west toward Fifth Avenue. Along the eastern wall of Central Park, the whole pack of us—father, mother, and four grown children— proceed in silence.

Arriving at the zoo, we follow a crowd of visitors through the gateway along a path around the administration building and through the Central Garden to the sea lions. We stand at the pool's edge watching the dark, submerged forms glide from end to end until another one of us says, "Let's go see the bears." So we go, following tree-lined paths to a fenced-in area of wooded terrain. The bears are nowhere in sight.

We keep walking, pausing by the penguins, making our way back to the Central Garden. We find a couple of park benches where we sit, each thinking some version of: *What now?* Each of us is silent in our shared dreamscape of birdcalls, children's voices, and emotions that take us to the edge of new and formidable territory. Being together like this—not knowing what to do next but free, for the moment, from any form of decision—lifts us out of the heavy, oppressive aftermath of our visit with the doctors. Something feels lighter, and we begin to discuss what to do about dinner.

Two days later, through a happenstance conversation, my mother learns about a doctor in Boston who does a minimally invasive version of the surgery. She makes an appointment for my father to meet him. I feel ambivalent. After our discouraging experience at one of New York City's "top" cancer treatment hospitals, I wonder if Boston's "internationally renowned" hospital will also have its share of arrogant doctors.

But my parents have spoken by phone with an older woman, a friend of a friend, who had the same procedure six months ago. The woman is eighty years old and is "doing great!" She has nothing but the highest praise for the surgeon and oncologist that my parents drive to Boston to meet. Sure enough, the appointment goes well and a date for surgery is set for mid-August, just a few weeks away.

Longing
to be present

longing to see
in the dark

can I turn
the light of my attention

toward
what is arising?

Six

My brothers and I make a plan to meet at the Boston hospital on the day of my father's surgery. The night before, my parents and I stay with my brother Ben and his family, just outside the city in Newton. Jeff also lives locally, farther north in Concord where John spends the night after flying in from France.

That evening at Ben's place, after a light dinner and attempts at casual conversation, my father says he's ready for bed. As our parents lay out their clothes for the next morning, Ben and I help them figure out what needs to go in my father's overnight bag. It's mostly an excuse to hang out with our parents and try to diffuse the waves of anxiety that they both are feeling. Out in the hallway, after coordinating our alarms for an early rising, I leave Ben and head upstairs to my nephew's room, since he's away at basketball camp.

Lying in bed with my worries for my father, I feel soothed by the room's soft blue walls and sports-themed décor. As I call upon the spirits and good graces of the unseen world, I feel strengthened by the poster images of famous athletes whose names I don't recognize. I'm grateful for their presence, their shadowy bodies in the dark, leaping and soaring overhead.

The next morning, Ben drives my mother, my father, and me through the rush hour traffic to the hospital where we meet Jeff and John who have driven in from Concord. We have plenty of time to go through the check-in routine. So many hallways, doorways, right turns, left turns, and then we come to the place where we expect to say goodbye to my father. Instead, we're invited to wait and join him shortly in the pre-op room. We wait until an aide arrives and leads us down another corridor through a set of swinging double doors. Then the aide stops, pulls back a curtain, and there's my father.

"You found me!" he says, as we form our familial circle around his gurney. The aide smiles and chats briefly with my father as the nurses assemble. Emboldened by the warm support of everyone we've met so far, I ask the nurses, "Can he keep his special, suede pouch with him?" It's filled with healing talismans from friends, and the medical team cheerily accommodates the request. A nurse points to the big toe of his right foot, and suggests we tie the pouch there so it won't be in the way.

A few minutes later, we are sent back through the maze of corridors to the waiting lounge where other families have also gathered. As we sit and wait, it is the acquiescing gesture of a nurse and the image of that small suede pouch on my father's toe that keeps me grounded through the long nine hours of my father's surgery. I've brought books to read, but mostly we talk, or take turns going outside to walk, to get lunch or a snack. We wait.

In my periodic wanderings around the hospital halls, I discover a door with an intriguing sign: "Renewal Room." I open the door and find what is clearly a sacred space. It is a calm, uncluttered, low-lit room, a place where staff, patients, and apparently family members, can meditate, reflect, or pray. No one else is here. I sit in one of the empty chairs.

The intentional care with which the room was created, holds me, supports me. Turning attention to my breath, I notice I'm barely breathing. Tightness is gripping my upper chest. With shoulders rising, I observe the sensation, a quality of being suspended. It's harder to name the emotion—it always is for me—but I recognize the contours, the inner bracing: *fear*. Again, I remember the quality of care we have met throughout the day. My mouth opens slightly; the exhale slowly, slowly comes. Everything becomes very still.

Here in the quiet, I know you are where you need to be.

The words arise and then vanish. I feel a softening in my chest and a gentle vibration flowing through my whole body and in the space around my body.

The boundary that separates us falls away.

Behind my closed eyes, in this moment of connection somehow shared with my father, an inner texture of light is moving.

Thy will be done.

It is evening when we get the call to join the surgeon in a family consulting room.

"All went well. Bob is in the recovery room," he tells us. "Pretty soon they'll have him ready to go to intensive care. You'll be able to see him some time tomorrow."

There is an audible communal sigh of relief. I watch the doctor's face, looking for signs of hidden meaning. He is patient with us and projects an aura of warm confidence. Even though the information he gives us is mostly general, I decide to believe him that all went well.

Then the doctor adds, "Often, after a long surgery, older patients may experience some confusion, but that is to be expected."

As my mother, brothers, and I head to the parking garage, we are mildly elated but mostly exhausted. Jeff and John come back to Ben's place for dinner. Before they leave to drive back to Concord, the four of us get out our calendars and devise a schedule so we can take turns visiting my father over the coming week. I've planned to stay for a couple of days before I head back home. After that, I'll drive up from Providence when I can.

Returning to my brother's house, reunited with the basketball stars on the walls of my nephew's bedroom, I call Jeremy and Julia to tell them about the day. I leave messages for Sam and Molly. Then lights out. Within minutes, I'm asleep.

The next morning, back at the hospital, my mother and I are instructed to wait outside the Intensive Care Unit. Two hours later, when we're allowed into my father's room, we find him stirring, still asleep, but starting to come in and out from the anesthesia and post-surgery meds. He wakes enough to recognize us and seems so happy we're here. His eyes open wide.

"I want to tell you about something I dreamed," he says. "First there was the dream of death." He pauses, and with some surprise, adds "And it was fine!"

I am leaning forward, so curious to hear more.

"And then there was the dream of birth—and it was spectacular!" He closes his eyes again and after a pause, says, "They really have it figured out. It all makes sense, and there is nothing to worry about."

As my father lies amidst a network of tubes, sharing his intriguing dreams, I feel a twinge of excitement—perhaps he has experienced something new and revelatory. Perhaps we will learn something of cosmic mystery! Perhaps he and I will be able to talk about spiritual phenomena.

Before I can ask him any questions, two nurses come into the room, and attention turns to medical matters. Afterwards, he is very tired and falls into a deep sleep.

A few hours later, when he wakes up again, I ask him if he wants to say anything more about the dreams.

"No," he answers brusquely.

In a conspiratorial whisper he adds, "The bus to North Carolina will be coming soon, and whatever you do, don't get on it!" I want to laugh but my father's dark tone is troubling. Clearly he is in a different state of mind than earlier, but soon he drifts back to sleep again.

My father is still sleeping when Ben arrives in the late afternoon to relieve my mother and me. Jeff and John join him after we've left. That evening, Ben and I compare notes—funny things Dad said: "The nurses are very good actors." "The hospital is wonderful, better than a church." Ben tells me that at one point my father asked him, "Do I have to stop drinking wine?"

"You haven't had any for a while," Ben answered.

"Oh no, am I dead?" asked my father.

By the next day, we are no longer laughing. My father knows who we, his family members, are, but everyone else—especially the doctors and nurses—belong, apparently, to a nefarious network of evildoers. He keeps trying to save us from their schemes. No one, it seems, can be trusted. But what is most distressing is that the rational, self-aware person we know so well is not here. Whose voice is this? These unmoored thoughts of his have a power that's urging my father to protect himself, to resist the efforts of his medical team. This is worse than anything we've dealt with in terms of the cancer. With everything else, we've been able to assume a shared sense of reality. Even when we've stumbled in our attempts to support him, he has always "been there" to accept or reject our support. Now we can't find him. I feel utterly helpless.

Over the next five days of his recovery in the ICU, it's hard to get any-one—nurses, doctors, even one of the hospital psychologists—to talk about what's happening. Apparently, what doctors euphemistically call *confusion* is actually a form of post-surgical psychosis that, for my fa-ther, includes paranoia and physical agitation—all of which, thankfully, begin to improve as his drug dosages are lowered and he is moved to another room away from the central hub of the ICU, where day and night, monitors glow red and green and beep in twenty-minute incre-ments. None of which, however, explains the transition from his state of wonder to his state of fear. Or why the dream of death preceded the dream of birth. Or where self-awareness goes when it's not at home in one's own body.

Moments and scenes from my father's two weeks in Boston slip and slide in time, punctuated by elevator rides to and from the hospital's eleventh floor. I travel back and forth from Providence, moving be-tween worlds. At the hospital, I am a visitor in a strange land. Even when I'm outside with my mother or brothers for lunch or a walk, all seems upended and precarious: the shrill sounds of ambulance sirens and people yelling, the hot days getting hotter, more uncomfortable. While stepping out of a coffee shop into an outdoor square, we see a man standing on top of a statue singing loudly and wordlessly to the sky. A crowd gathers and firemen arrive to talk him down.

Then comes the news that Ted Kennedy has died. On the day of his funeral at the nearby Basilica of Our Lady of Perpetual Help, streets are closed and traffic backs up all around the hospital. A mood of mourning prevails over the city. It is such a relief when September finally comes and my father can return home.

Back and forth. Instead of traveling to Boston, most weekends I go to Stamford where the "library" room at my parents' house has become a makeshift infirmary. One evening, after they've gone to bed, I take a little time for myself. A high-pitched fatigue resides behind my eyes, above my sternum, and all around the right side of my head. I light a candle and close my eyes to see what else I might learn.

Arms rise overhead, wrists turning in the rising. Wanting to stretch. Reaching.

In this space above my head, reaching fingers soften and my hands begin to slowly, slowly lower. The slowness is just right. I have such a longing for this tempo in my life. It's like existing in a completely different atmosphere, enveloping me gently, like warm air. Coiling smoke rises from the wick when I blow out the candle, reminding me of my curling, rising wrists as they reached overhead to the heavens. Rising hands, seeking answers: What happens in a mind? What is happening in my father's mind?

Confundo. The Latin source for the word confusion means to *mingle*. Another benign word that barely begins to shed light on my father's post-surgical state of mind. Meld, mix, merge, mayhem. Henry Miller wrote, "Confusion is a word we have invented for an order which is not yet understood."[21] Calling confusion an "order," Miller implies that it's a natural outcome of a sequence of events. I find this helpful. For my father, the events culminated in the ICU—his body under siege from cancer, chemo, surgery, and medication; his mind, emerging from anesthesia. Everything, mingling and jumbled, became focused on defending against this latest and most extreme assault.

My mother is a tireless caregiver, encouraging, even impelling my father toward wellness. Still recovering from the surgery, he has a portable IV to keep fluids pumping through him. He is gaining strength and mobility but sometimes the confusion returns. One day, as I'm sitting with him, he is staring at the IV.

"Why is this sand pouring into me?" he asks.

After a long pause, he turns to me and says, "That's the confusion talking, right?"

"Yes," I say, inwardly rejoicing as I recognize the voice of his inner witness. Self-knowing and discernment are back. My father is home again, here in himself.

The air is cooling, and most mornings are quite crisp. Back in Providence, Mariposa, once again, consumes my attention. We opened our first official pre-Kindergarten classroom, seventeen eager children, lucky winners of the state lottery, have joined us. One more child still to come. A couple of families have already told us they are unable to accept the spot because of a lack of transportation. I keep calling the phone number for the girl who is next in line on our waiting list. Each time I dial, it's with an urgent desire to reach this family and welcome them to Mariposa, but there is no answer. I keep calling for a couple of days, then drive to their address. A woman sees me looking for the right door at the multi-family house and wants to know what I'm doing. When I ask if she knows the family, she tells me they no longer live here.

We need to move on to the next name on the waiting list. But why is my failure to find this little girl so unsettling? Why do I feel that I am personally participating in this missed opportunity? The whole system of gaining one's education through a lottery ticket seems terribly twisted. The perversity of institutionalized randomness is no way to lead a country into the future. Fate's fortune is unpredictable enough.

But it's more than a stand against the facelessness of the lottery wheel. Whatever intuition is, I feel it here, a soundless calling from the future, compelling me to find this particular child, telling me she belongs with this group of children who are assembling by the good graces of chance to inaugurate the Mariposa Pre-K.

We call the next two names on the waiting list. Both are boys. But it's already October: The families have made arrangements they don't want to change. Before calling the family of the third name on the list, I again try the number for the little girl we couldn't find. This time someone answers. It's the girl's aunt. Their phone was turned off for a few weeks, but their service started up again yesterday. The girl's mother calls back an hour later.

"I can't believe it! Yes, yes, yes," she practically cries. "Please save that last spot for us! Thank you!"

And that is how the eighteenth child arrives. When I visit the classroom a few weeks later and see her for the first time, she is deeply and happily immersed in play, surrounded by her new friends. Four of them are creating an elaborate meal. One child carries a cooking pot back and forth from the beautifully set table to the "kitchen," while another pours an invisible liquid into four cups.

I wonder what impact this year will have on each of these boys and girls—such a formative age. Watching the children, I can hardly believe the vision has become manifest. A small-scale avenue of possibility that meets my deep longing for every child to be welcomed with the opportunity to develop in the fullest way possible.

Later, while on a break in my teaching studio at the top of the old Victorian, I remember being about the same age as the Mariposa children, thinking that I had the power to make myself invisible. One long-ago Saturday in autumn, I was with my mother visiting a friend of hers. While the adults chatted over tea, I was encouraged to play with the woman's son in the backyard.

Standing shyly under a tree, I watch the boy swing a baseball bat around and around over his head. I look away, across the garden, wondering what to do. I look back just as the bat comes flying at my face, hitting my left eye.

Memory jumps a day. I am at school and the teacher, bending down, is looking closely at me.

"What happened to your eye?" she asks.

In a flash, I knew if I pretended nothing was wrong, then that's what the teacher would see.

"Nothing," I say.

With complete conviction, I believed I could make myself, my wound, my vulnerabilities, invisible. Of course, it didn't work. The teacher called my parents to arrange a meeting. But that didn't change my inclination to want to disappear. It was an ability I cultivated as I got older and deployed in moments of discomfort and self-consciousness, especially with anyone outside my immediate family.

Perhaps, as an introspective child, I internalized my parents' well-intentioned insistence that "it's nothing" and "don't worry, no one will make a big deal about it." In my little-girl version of reality there was no distinction between my experience and the teacher's experience. At that age, I could not conceive of our experience as being separate. The incident would mark a nascent awareness that how others see me is not how I see myself, and that how I see myself is not the whole story. There are always blind spots, things we can't know or see, and sometimes there are gaps in awareness, the places where we separate from our own experience.

The blank space between being hit by the bat and my return to school is exactly this sort of lacuna, a big empty space of no memory. I feel it now as the absence of something I can't quite make out. I close my eyes and the absence feels endless, no beginning, no ending. Staying with the feeling, eyes squeezing shut, my mouth opens with no sound, and absence becomes something I recognize as shock. Then comes an image-like feeling of falling. I know there must be pain but mostly, I feel numb. I see myself being helped off the ground, walking into the house, guided by a hand on my shoulder, escorted by the numbness.

Through the decades, it is the numbness that has stayed with me, arising to accompany me through the next unexpected incident. In a subtle way it is with me now, like a guardian, as I think of my father's diagnosis and all that he is going through. This time, as I sit in my studio, I let the silent sentinel be here. I feel my stillness, my raised shoulders, my barely moving breath. My eyes are squinting, wanting to squeeze shut, not wanting to see what may be coming.

A conversation unfolds, compassion speaks softly:

> You don't have to be afraid to see what's coming.
> You don't have to be afraid of not knowing.

I silently repeat these words to my shoulders, to my breath, to my eyes. A softening spreads through my body bringing, at least for this moment, a sense of ease.

October becomes November. The days are getting downright cold and most of the leaves have fallen from the trees. Across a busy road at the end of my street is a small cemetery that leads into Roger Williams Park, Providence's oldest and largest public park. It's an urban pastoral landscape with tall trees, grassy slopes, and a series of interconnecting ponds. The park, for me, is a haven of consolation.

Today, I head toward a grove of old maple trees standing tall and wide. Drawn to the bareness of the branches, I stop to see their dark, skeletal forms against the cloud-white light of the overcast sky. Their rooted stillness and their upward reach somehow comfort me.

My father continues to get stronger and the moments of confusion become rare. My parents have a new primary care physician, who is engaged, knowledgeable, and seems willing to be a guide and advocate. The difference this makes for them is remarkable. There is now someone to turn to who knows how to navigate the course of illness, who cares to ask my parents how they are doing and who, above all, inspires confidence that we are on the right path.

Confidence, from the Latin, *fid,* to have trust in, to have faith. The first time I meet Dr. Fred, as he urges us to call him, and watch him interact with my father, I want to fall to the ground in gratitude. There is, of course, no guarantee that he can save my father, and yet, here is a doctor who has the compassion of a witness. For all of us, trust and faith in my father's process has been renewed.

Eyes close...

descending
into body
meeting what's moving
or still

finding feeling
maybe fear
maybe joy
or something nameless
within a gesture
sensation or rhythm

following
where it goes

What is here?

SEVEN

When we were growing up, there was one group that my brothers and I knew was not part of the "*we*" our father liked to remind us are "all on the same side." My father's most reactive moments were reserved for religious institutions, especially "the Church." While he raised a family, his views evolved, softening with regard to individuals who he thought should be free to have their own beliefs. What grew stronger, over time, was his concern regarding the phenomenon of *certitude*. The unabashed conviction that one's beliefs are unassailably right and therefore to be heeded and applied universally.

My mother was raised Catholic and my father's family was Presbyterian. When I was a child, the ramifications of that difference always shocked me. I couldn't fathom how my mother's parents could disown their daughter and future son-in-law just because they refused to sign a document promising to raise their children in the Roman Catholic tradition.

Even now, it's difficult for me to imagine my very competent and secure parents abandoned in this way in their early twenties. My father's mother had been quite sick for a number of years, and my mother's mother was an alcoholic—neither was equipped to be emotionally available for either of my parents. It was a friend of my father's family, Helen, who responded to the plight of the young couple, offering to host a wedding reception as if it were for one of her own children.

To me, this story has always felt like the creation myth of my family. For my parents, as they began to make a life far from their families of origin, Helen inspired an impulse to make family out of friends, to forge new connections and support systems wherever they lived. After I was born, my parents named Helen as my godmother. The role was meant as a symbolic gesture, but for Helen it was a relationship she took seriously. Over the years I only saw her the few times we went to Chicago to visit my grandparents, but she wrote to me every birthday and Christmas for forty years until she died. The last few cards came in Braille after she had lost most of her sight.

Helen's mostly invisible presence in my life as a child was oversized. Her effortless benevolence reflected a certain mood of the larger mystery that I couldn't see yet felt was just beyond the physical dimensions of my world. The very fact of having a godmother was an embodiment of something spiritual I yearned to know more about. Growing up in an atmosphere of ambivalence toward organized religion, we celebrated Christmas and Easter in the secular way of Christian holidays: ornaments, presents, Easter baskets, and egg hunts. Until I was eight years old, I had never been in a church.

It started with a gift. My mother's parents had come for a rare visit and my grandmother, intent to focus all of her redemption efforts on me, had asked me to come help her unpack because she had something to give me. I watched her open her suitcase and reach under her folded blouses and rolled balls of beige stockings for a small, white box. Inside was a fancy necklace that my grandmother told me was very special.

"It's a rosary," she said. "You can pray with it."

The next day, when she invited me to go with her to Sunday Mass, I felt special—none of my brothers had been invited—though not entirely comfortable. My grandmother scared me. She had a brassy presence, wore a lot of make-up, and I didn't like having so much attention on me. But I was curious about the church business: What would it be like? For one thing, I was instructed to dress up in my best clothes, my nicest spring outfit: a red cotton dress with a white collar, white knee socks, and black patent leather shoes. My grandmother had brought me a new pair of white gloves for the occasion. I didn't want to wear them but I put them on.

The two of us walked together out of the bright sunshine through a huge wooden doorway, into darkness. My grandmother steered me by the elbow down an aisle until we stopped at one of the rows of people. When they stood to let us pass, we squeezed by them to find a seat. The bench was hard, everyone sat up straight. I took off the white gloves so I could feel the soft roundness of the rosary beads passing between my fingers as I sat in the pew. Everything was dark and contained within the large, domed interior. I felt very small. I couldn't see what anyone was doing. I couldn't comprehend what the priest was saying and I didn't know what I was supposed to do.

Church was not at all what I had expected. However, two years later, when I was in fourth grade, I discovered something I could fully embrace. Every Monday throughout the school year, our teacher began the week with a story from the Hebrew Bible, or as we called it then, the Old Testament. By the time we got to Joseph, his colorful coat, mean brothers, prophetic dreams, and innate gifts recognized, I was completely besotted. One Saturday afternoon, searching through every bookcase in our house, I found what I was looking for—the royal blue box holding the Bible that had been a gift for me from my godmother Helen when I was born. With Bible tucked under my shirt, I snuck down the basement stairs, taking me out of sight and below the busy hum of life in the rest of the house.

Sitting on the rumpled couch, I opened the box and found a gold paper-covered box within. I carefully lifted the lid and took out the small, white, leather-bound book. The print was so tiny I didn't even try to read any of the stories. I just turned the pages. On the dedication page, I found my name. Below were empty spaces waiting for names and dates of family marriages, births, and deaths. Maps of "The Ancient World" were placed at the end of the book, and a thin white ribbon nestled within the pages of text marking the separation of the Old and New Testaments. Just as I was pondering this last detail, I heard someone coming down the stairs. It was my father. I slammed the book shut as if caught with something nasty and forbidden.

We never spoke about this. I don't even know if my father saw what I had been holding. I do remember putting the book away in its double boxes and returning it to the bookshelf. After that, it wasn't the stories that stirred me as I lay falling asleep at nights: rather, my brief turning of the gold-edged pages had confirmed a mystery that had greatly puzzled me.

As every child in Toronto who attended public schools in the mid-1960s knew, people and events took their respective place on either side of B.C. and A.D. You didn't have to go to church to know this. Every morning, our teachers wrote the letters A.D. at the end of the day's date on the top right-hand corner of the classroom blackboard.

Who had decided we would mark a zero point of time, a place between everything prior flowing backward into time receding and everything subsequent flowing forward into an always and forever unfolding present?

And what, I wondered as I remembered the thin white satin ribbon, *is in the space between before and after?*

The spiritual longings of my childhood continue to live in the intangible realm of the will, the most unconscious and mystifying of our inner capacities. Will manifests as impulse, movement, intended action, unintended action, volition, and agency. Even inaction can be an act of will. All of this is what first attracted me to the Discipline of Authentic Movement, where movement and stillness, the signatures of impulse, are central to the practice.

Longing itself is an expression of will, an intuitive impulse seeking to become more of who one is. Call it human striving. Call it a quest, quiet and inward. My quest to understand the relationship between *will* and *time* becomes more personal when I think of my father. His will to live is a discernable force, day-by-day driving forward, regardless of what the cancer or treatment throws at him. In this sense, his will to live seems inseparable from the stream of time, emerging as one unstoppable flow. Suddenly, death seems all the more stunning, all the more aberrant. How does such a powerful force just stop?

Thankfully, my father is not stopping. My mother's frequent emails report that my father is feeling better, more mobile, and able to eat a greater variety of real food. But in spite of the upbeat prognosis, I'm unable to shake a feeling of foreboding. It's been a grueling year since my father's diagnosis. I remember last December when my parents came to stay with us in Rhode Island for the holidays. Amidst the hubbub of the annual festivities, I vaguely noticed that my father was not eating much, leaving his usual favorite foods—the herb-roasted lamb, crusty bread, sautéed broccoli with garlic—while picking at the softer food like pasta and sweet potatoes. It was an observation that quickly receded to the shadowy recesses of my awareness.

On the last evening of the visit, my father said he was getting tired. While he was in the bathroom washing up and putting on pajamas, I opened the sofa bed in the room my parents were sleeping in.

"Let me help you," he said, returning from the bathroom.

"I think we're all set," I answered as I lay an extra blanket at the bottom of the pulled-out bed.

Wearing a pair of loose navy shorts and a T-shirt, my father walked to his side of the bed. Shocked by how skinny he looked, I puttered around, moving throw pillows, folding a sweater, until he was lying down.

"Dad, are you feeling okay?" I asked.

"Yeah. I'm fine," he said. "I'm just tired."

I didn't say anything. No one was saying anything. *Everything is fine.* If I don't see something, it's not happening.

Less than a month later, he received the diagnosis of esophageal cancer. My father had been in pain and unable to eat; why had he waited so long to tell us? Why had we waited so long to notice?

It's nearing the end of January, over a year since those days of denial. We're in a cold stretch here in Rhode Island, but I try to walk in the park every few days, following the path that snakes along the water's edge from one pond to the next. One day I stop to watch a falling leaf take a detour from gravity, riding slant-ways down a pillow of air. I wait for it to touch ground, but too light to land, the leaf skitters across the icy pond, vanishing. Nothing left but these words. This sense of not landing is with me all the time. Where's the ground?

A few nights later, I'm wide awake until dawn, unable to lay down the busyness of mind, the whir of body. In the fatigue of the next day, surrender finally comes. I lie on the floor and there is nothing here but the weight of my body. Too tired to think, too worn out to resist what I need which is, in fact, to do nothing.

The sensation of heaviness is all I can register until the physical sensations begin to well up, becoming the rheumy weight of grief. Even more than grief, what's here is the feeling of not wanting *to feel* the grief. I don't want to lose my father. I don't want to begin to feel what it will be like to let him go.

Days and weeks pass in a blur of thawing and freezing under leaden skies, a perpetual dreariness. February and March come and go. In early April, my father returns to his oncologist in Boston. It is a late afternoon appointment so my parents decide to take the train. After meeting with the doctor, they plan to spend the night at Ben's place and take the train home the next day.

That night, Ben calls me.

"The cancer is back," he says. "It's in his lungs, but it's not lung cancer. The doctor says it's still considered esophageal cancer."

I ask Ben what happens now. He says that the doctor wants my father to try a different chemo for four weeks, followed by a two-week break from treatment. Then they'll do a PET scan to see if there's any change.

When I talk with my parents, my father says he's disappointed, but he sounds determined to stay positive: "They have a new treatment for me." He puts the emphasis on "treat" as if it's something special the pharmacists have whipped up just for him. My mother doesn't say much about the doctor visit, but she tells me about the horrendous over-sold train ride up to Boston. "There were no seats! Your father and I had to sit on our bags." I am sure, like me, she is devastated.

Six weeks later, we all meet in Boston with the oncologist to review the results of the scan. My parents drove there together, I drove from Providence, John flew in from Paris while Ben and Jeff coordinated our convergence at the medical center. No matter what the report tells us, the plan is that I will drive my father home and spend the week with him. My mother will continue on, driving to Vermont, where she will lead a weeklong meditation retreat. My father tells us that he feels good, is pain-free, and stronger than he's felt in months. I am apprehensive but join the collective mood of optimism.

The doctor wastes no time. As soon as we're all seated, he looks directly at each of us and says, "There's no other way to say it; it's not good news. The new round of chemotherapy isn't working."

His words are emphatic but spoken with care and compassion. I feel stunned. The room is silent. The doctor gives us time to let the news settle. Can I let myself feel the great sadness of this? Can I be present with my father for what he needs? Can we meet what's here and what's coming? I don't know.

I glance at my father and see, for the first time, defeat.

It doesn't stay for long. After some discussion in response to the doctor's questions about my father's general health and energy, my father asks, "Okay, what do we do now?"

Promising to follow up with a possible lead to participate in a clinical trial, the doctor ends the appointment with a modicum of hope. We file back out into the late morning sunlight. My brothers have meetings to get to. My father and I say goodbye to my mother and get in my car for the drive back to Stamford.

With my father's typical foresight, assuming we would get back too late to shop for dinner, he has made a reservation for us at a favorite restaurant in New Haven. After a quiet ride, we arrive two hours before the restaurant opens. This is a minor obstacle; he has no intention of changing the plan. We decide to park the car and walk around until the restaurant opens.

On this warm spring afternoon, the street is filled with people walking on the sunny side. Passing through a stone doorway onto the Yale campus, my father and I are together, yet we each follow our own path. We are not really talking, just walking and looking around. My heart keeps pace with his. I'm not thinking about where we are going, I just want to give him space while I soak in every moment with him.

Crossing the long and narrow central green, we step around students and avoid airborne soccer balls and Frisbees. We follow a small group of visitors into a building where an arched corner entry beckons. In the middle of a room that has a pale blue domed ceiling, we stop. The other visitors continue on.

My father is looking up, his mouth barely open with that expression of wonder he gets, as if he's a child and the world is telling him a story. Maybe he's never walked to the middle of an oval room with a ceiling the color of sky and stood still, at least not this room, certainly not this moment. I let it wash over me, this feeling of wonder that he exudes, this openness to a world that is worth paying attention to in its every ordinary moment. I cherish this brief interlude of witnessing him still alive and so present to his surroundings, even on this day of learning that he's going to die. But not yet, we still have a dinner reservation to get to.

He orders oysters—forbidden food according to the blood-type diet recommendations. He only eats a couple. We both poke at the rest of the lovely food without much appetite. It is hard to know what to say. It had been so much simpler when we were walking wordlessly, better to keep moving. We ask our waiter to put our dinner in containers to go. It's a relief when we are outside again, feeling the cooler evening air, walking to the car, getting back on the road, following the white lines as the night darkens, returning to the comfort and familiarity of home.

The days continue to be sunny and warm. We try to spend as much time outside as possible. One afternoon, we are sitting in the garden; my father is pursing his lips, trying to practice projecting his voice, but the blowing sounds seem thin, bodiless. He's discouraged about this. Over the years, whenever he expresses interest, I tell him about the Alexander Technique, and show him how to be more aware of his head balanced on top of his spine, creating more space and ease in his joints.

We're side by side, stretched out on lawn chairs. I encourage him to experiment with not doing anything, not trying to speak, just following the inhale, exhale, inhale of his breath, feeling his vocal cords vibrate when he hums. No effort required, only gentle attention to what's happening. When he does this, the sound changes.

"I can hear it from the inside!" he says. Then we're quiet for a while, sitting in the warm afternoon light. His eyes are closed.

He agrees to experiment with "seeing what's here." I suggest it as a way to be in the present moment and notice what's here in the garden, but he takes the prompt in another direction, gazing out with a faraway look. I ask what he sees.

"I see an elephant," he says, pointing toward the neighboring yard, "over in that space between the bushes." His voice is soft and dreamy: "It's tucking its trunk under its ear and around to its tail. It's taking its time, but it's getting ready to leave."

Does he know what he is saying? I turn toward him, searching his face for a clue. His eyes are closed again. He looks peaceful. I lay back in the reclining chair. The sun's enveloping warmth softens the shock of his words, but I know the metaphor is true. And there is nothing I can do about it.

When our children were young, Jeremy's grandmother stayed with us every couple of months for a week at a time. His grandfather had died two years earlier, and Gram was not happy about living on without him. She and I often ate lunch together and talked about death and the afterlife.

"I'm not religious," she once said, "but I believe in God. I talk to God every day, but I never get an answer."

Another time she told me about a game she often played when she was by herself. She would look at something long enough for it to become something else, and then it began, in her mind, to speak. She described, for example, sitting in our backyard, staring at the tall tomato stakes in the garden until they turned into an alternating sequence of *Yes/No/Yes/No/Yes/No*. She would count up and down the rows of stakes to get an answer to her question: "Will I die soon?" She tried this mental exercise a few different ways—left to right, right to left, skipping every other stake—always slightly disappointed when the answer came out *No*.

Some might call this projection, but to me, Gram was a colleague in the animation laboratory of the mind, creating ritual out of perception. When I suggested she was bringing things to life, she replied, "I don't know about that, but it brings me to life!" I asked if she thought her game was, in fact, a conversation with God. I suggested that maybe *this is* how God speaks to her, through the gift of her imagination. She wasn't sure about that either.

My father is in the house resting, while I'm still here in the garden remembering the elephant in the bushes, hoping the time it takes to leave will be long.

Out of the silence
comes a voice
you can speak or write
words
that stay close
to body
and feeling

EIGHT

Defying the forecast of showers, the afternoon is sunny and warm as my father and I take a walk in nearby Cove Island, a vibrant city park not far from my parents' house. Everyone is moving faster than we are—joggers, mothers pushing strollers, kids on skateboards, and rollerbladers—but that's okay, we're starting our second loop of the mile-long walking path. My father says he's feeling good but soon he stops and asks, "Would you mind if we take a short rest on the bench here?"

As usual, we're facing water, a narrow estuary that leads from Long Island Sound to Holly Pond. We watch the gulls. One, airborne, is shrieking at another standing on the shoreline. We watch people pass. I love that we can be here, so comfortably, without speaking, just noticing what's happening around us, though there is still so much I want to talk about with my father. I decide to ask for his best advice on bringing a vision to reality: "How do you make something out of nothing but an idea?"

"The most important thing," he begins, "is you get the best people you can."

I ask him what he means by the best.

"Well, the best isn't just about being smart, although that helps. No, the best is about certain qualities. It's a combo of smarts, an enthusiasm and openness to life and all that it brings, and a deep capacity to care about other people and to care about how the job gets done. And woven through all of that are two essential characteristics, humor and humility."

"That's great, but it isn't always easy to find people with these qualities, even when you're looking for them," I say.

"Unless you're looking in Canada," he says with a grin. "When we lived in Toronto, I always deeply appreciated the humor and humility of Canadians."

And with that, we continue walking on, sharing memories of the Toronto years until we're approaching the end of the loop. I know this, without looking, because whenever the end is in sight, my father speeds up. After easing along at our slow, ambling pace, I have to hustle to keep up with him. We pass a jogger on her cool-down walk and make our way through the parking lot back to the car and home again for a late afternoon rest.

The week with my father is coming to an end. The night before my mother returns, I stay up late turning the pages of *Anticancer*, a book my mother has urged me to read. I fall asleep with the firm resolve to convince my father to think anew about the foods that heal and the foods that enable tumors. Maybe it's not too late to starve the cancer into submission.

In the morning, we're in the kitchen together. I bring out two small, sealed cups of sea cucumber jelly from the refrigerator, as instructed by my mother. I offer to eat one in solidarity with him. "What's the point?" he asks. This has been his same response each of the last few mornings. I open the book and read a passage.

With little visible enthusiasm, he unseals the cup, picks up a spoon, and scoops the murky, brown liquid into his mouth. I open my portion and down it. It's not bad. It's not good, but not bad. I tell him what I'm making us for breakfast—oatmeal with raisins, a little granola, sunflower and hemp seeds, all chopped finely.

While it cooks, my father looks up and says, "I want to get..." It takes him a moment to remember the word. "...Buttermilk!"

And then he describes the wonders of buttermilk pancakes in great detail. This is definitely not part of the meal regimen that my mother has entrusted me with.

"Too bad I can't have the dairy," I say, diverting the idea of buttermilk pancakes.

I serve the oatmeal and we both agree it tastes good. But then, as I'm washing the breakfast dishes, he turns to me with great intensity and says, "Sauerkraut and duck!" Light shines from his eyes. They are so blue and alive in this moment. And I know I will go with him to find every ingredient we need, from the cabbage to the juniper berries on the bush out back, and then we'll cook the duck in the Dutch oven. Even the way he says "Dutch oven" tells me that this is a life-affirming project. It's only when he mentions, with a kind of awe, "duck fat," that he sees me hesitate.

"Oh no," he assures me, "duck fat has far more vitamins than chicken fat." I pretend to believe him.

Turns out we don't actually need to prepare any of it. It's enough that I've joined him in the imagining of this meal. We move on with the day, both of us feeling, it seems, quite nourished. It's fascinating to me how the imagining of a meal or an adventure or, really, any experience can convey the essence of the lived experience. The same vivid imagination that allows my father to bring ideas to reality allows him to experience some of the benefits of an idea, even if it doesn't come to fruition.

After I pack my bags in anticipation of my mother's return, I join my father outside where he sits, reading a book. I stretch out on the deck chair next to him. The shore birds are busy feeding in the shoals of the Sound while clouds drift lazily across the sky. I am about to ask if the tide is coming in or going out, when I feel my father's eyes on my arm. He is looking intently at my watch and I realize he's not happy with the new watch we recently bought for him. This is when we trade.

As we each take off our watches, I feel in unison with my father. Our movements have the sense of ritual, concentrating time and space into the wholeness of what's here right now. Nothing else is happening, just this.

I help my father put my watch on his left wrist and then I put his watch on my left wrist. Everything that has happened has led up to this. Everything that must continue will follow this. We are in the timeless space between before and after.

I drive home through the dark wearing my father's watch. The highway is mostly empty so my thoughts roam freely, reviewing everything that has happened over the past year, and all that is changing. By the time I cross into Rhode Island, there is nothing more to think. For the rest of the way, mercifully, my mind is quiet.

The next morning, Julia and I plan to take a walk at the end of the day. After she arrives home from school, we make our way into the park, down to the path along the pond. The gnats are doing their dance at the water's edge, where the trees gesture with their budding green branches. Julia carries the sadness of a recent break-up. I'm touched by how open and available she seems.

Tomorrow we'll make the two-hour drive to meet Molly one more time before she graduates. We'll go to a mall and find dresses for the girls—Molly needs one for graduation, and Julia needs one for prom. None of us can believe that Molly, my parents' first grandchild, will soon complete college. Where did the time go? Meanwhile Sam is halfway through college and has had an exciting year with his baseball team winning their league title. Seeded #1, the team is competing in the regional playoffs, so Jeremy and I have spent the past few days driving to Willimantic to watch the games hosted at Eastern Connecticut College. As the timing gods would have it, the championship game begins at 5:00 p.m. on the Saturday before Molly's Sunday morning graduation. Jeremy will be the family representative cheering Sam and the team on, while the rest of us, including my father and Molly's five other grandparents, will celebrate with her at a graduation dinner.

On top of everything else, Jeremy and I are starting to build a new home on land we bought a few years ago. It's thirty-five minutes outside of Providence in a small rural town. We began planning for the next phase of our lives well before my father's illness; Jeremy is eager to stay on schedule and promises that he will be our project manager.

I find myself amazed that everything doesn't just stop so we can focus on my father. I wish I could stop time. I want everyone to stop everything they're doing so I can focus on him without feeling torn between being with him and being with my husband and children. But time doesn't care about me. Life goes on and so much is happening.

As my father navigates his way between illness and relative states of well-being, Mariposa is beginning its life within a world of young families. Our first year of offering Pre-K has gone miraculously well. A small group of founding board members have overseen the program and, with the help of a part-time business administrator, have begun the process of developing a non-profit organization. My co-founder, Linda Atamian, is working with the teachers to align everything they're doing with the state's early learning standards. And now, the board has decided to hire a half-time director. She will take over much of the administrative work Linda and I have shared this year.

After a bumpy start with finding the right teachers, we now have three devoted educators who are doing beautiful work with the children and families. Each of them is an inspiring presence. They are the kind of teachers that the children, when they're grown, will remember with love. In the words of Einstein, who had strong opinions about education: "The only rational way of educating is to be an example."

In the first seven years of life, the inner drive to grow and learn is an unconscious, will-based phenomenon. All of the child's developmental milestones emerge naturally through movement: rolling, crawling, standing upright, walking, and speaking. Along with movement, imitation and imagination are the main portals through which the young child learns. Children soak in everything around them. The early childhood classroom is the one place where *everything* a teacher says and does, for better or worse, is teaching the students something. The Mariposa teachers are discovering that their own gestures and movement, their tone of voice, are part of the children's educational environment.

The teachers talk a lot about the relationship between activity and receptivity, not just in terms of the child's will, but also in terms of their own. When the children are in a more active mode, such as when they're in deep play, the teacher is in a more receptive mode, stepping back, perhaps embodying the role of witness, ready to support or facilitate as needed, but not actively engaging or directing the play. Other times the teacher is more actively leading so the children are in a more receptive mode, either listening or imitating. This dynamic rhythm, along with an attuned awareness of the seasons and time of year, influences how the Mariposa teachers plan the day, the week, and their curriculum. This promotes a natural, organic approach to learning. It's creative and demanding work.

I've been meeting with the teachers, helping them become more aware of themselves in body and space, more aware of what arises in them in the presence of the children. I'm inspired by how they challenge themselves to stay open and receptive when observing the children without, if possible, making premature interpretations and judgments about the children's behavior and abilities. I ask the teachers what is different in the children's experience from their own.

"They live in the moment," one teacher says, and the others agree. "They're not consciously dwelling on the past or worried about the future. The present moment is everything for them."

Children have a very different relationship to time than adults. A child's thinking, feeling, and perceiving isn't so separate from their physical body. Inner self-awareness has not become divided from self-being. As adults, we've developed the gifts of reflective self-awareness, so we are capable of making conscious choices based on past experience and future goals. The cost of this ability is that we tend to be detached from our first-hand experience of sense, feeling, and intuition.

What the Mariposa teachers want to learn is how to meet the children where they are, in the moment, while still achieving their curriculum goals and keeping the classroom activities moving along. What does *being in the moment* mean for adults? We are learning that contemplative and embodied practices can help us experience this—presence as an enlivening relational awareness—without sacrificing our reflective capacities or regressing to places of arrested development.

My father excels at being in the moment as an adult. I wonder how he has cultivated this capacity. It seems he becomes more and more of who he is, whether alone or with others. When I experience myself in his presence, I feel more present. The curtain of self falls away and there we are in a shared moment of possibility.

Spring will soon be summer. Molly and the Mariposa five-year-olds have graduated, and are moving on to a job and to kindergarten, respectively. I feel a peculiar blend of sadness and elation. Maybe this is how it will always be for me whenever something ends and something new begins. Every time I see my father, I enter this same blurry terrain,

92

never knowing exactly what is ending and what is beginning, or which way the meld of feelings will tilt next.

Once again, I am back on the highway; once again, I am crossing the Gold Star Memorial Bridge over the Thames River, passing New London, Waterford, Old Lyme, then crossing the Connecticut River. The music of Thelonious Monk accompanies me—"Blue Hawk" over the Gold Star Bridge, the lyrical "Pannonica," through Old Lyme. Nothing in the world reminds me more of my father than the solo sound of Monk. Forget the classic duets with Coltrane, Mulligan, Blakey, or the fabulous quartets and quintets, it's Thelonious alone who does it. When it's just him and the piano, with an expanded space to play in, single notes have more room to extend. Runs set against a lone key let the one-off notes float. You can hear the creative activity of his mind in the moment of playing, the way he lets rhythm and melody converse. You have to get wider to stay in time with Monk. You can't help it, if you're really listening.

His cadence perfectly fits my father, who has been known to spend hours at the piano working the hesitations, letting the notes trip and stutter over each other, jabbing a key or two or more for emphasis, leaving unexpected spaces between notes. It occurs to me that this is just how my father thinks. He has a way of speaking with prolonged pauses, where you can't predict what the next word will be, so there's no point in rushing to fill the silence with your assumptions. Sometimes people get impatient with this trait of his, but the payoff for letting my father's thoughts find their own way to words is usually worth it.

I arrive at my parents' house and step out of the car. The air is muggy with the promise of imminent rain. Inside the house, my father tells me he has decided to undergo a procedure on his vocal cords where they are being impinged by a tumor. His voice is soft and reedy. It's increasingly hard to hear him and now he wearily anticipates not being able to speak for what the doctors predict will be several weeks. I suggest (again) that maybe he will want to write in one of the empty journals I keep buying for him. Maybe now, as practice and fun, he wants to write a poem?

He doesn't want to write a poem but agrees to speak about what he is experiencing; I can be the scribe, recording his words in a poem-like format. In a whisper, he speaks each line with a pause in between:

I can never write a poem
but the flowers follow me from room to room
now sitting here at home
the truth seeps through
I can never write a poem.

That's it.
My throat is sore
I have too many pills
I don't know
I don't know
No more lines to the poem.

Thus begins a period of weeks when my father cannot talk. He communicates his thoughts and questions on pads of paper. Some of the messages he writes are lists of activities he wants to fill the day with. Each activity has a corresponding note: *bikes: tuned up; paddle: hi-tide approx. 2pm; swim: fine/80° water; Wimbledon tennis: later*. When he puts them in order of preference, kayaking is always first on the list, walking is always last.

One day, while we are sitting at the kitchen table, I show him an article about how money and power affect the relationship between culture and nature. He reads every word, takes it in deeply, picks up his white pad of paper, and writes:

Paula
When I can talk freely
Let's return to this topic
Which under various headings I have wrestled
with for many years e.g. the constituencies of a
corporation using corporate bonus plans to influence
corporate culture components of corporate culture
etc.

He finishes his thought with the gesture of a spontaneous, self-designed symbol. This is what it looks like—a line under the words extending to the right of etc., the downward squiggle, becoming an arrow into empty space.

I stare at the wobbly line and the empty space, feeling an intimation of loss. The conversations that will never be. I stick the note among my papers. Later, looking at it again, I see the note and squiggling arrow as his form of poetry, his vision and his longing for a transformed corporate culture worthy of democracy and human dignity. A seed-thought for the future.

Empty page
empty space
waiting

again, waiting
listening
for an impulse

moving, being moved
seeing, being seen
may we be present enough
may we surrender enough

NINE

Bright blue sky and the staccato of firecrackers. It's Saturday morning on Fourth of July weekend at my parents' house, which will soon be overflowing with visiting family. The inquiry into other medical options for my father continues, but for now he is feeling good with renewed energy. His voice is stronger and he's been off chemo for a while. When I arrive, he's glad to have a kayaking partner again, so after lunch he and I set off into the full waters of high tide. As we round the corner past the neighbor's house and approach the bridge that crosses from the main road to a small island, my father lifts his legs over either side of the kayak, letting them dangle in the water. I can see this makes the craft less stable but I figure my father knows what he's doing. We're drifting under the bridge, when my father leans toward the piling on his left and falls into the water. Quelling panic, I maneuver myself alongside his kayak and by wedging it between a large rock and one of the bridge's steel standings, we are able to get him back on board. We decide not to proceed into the rougher waters on the other side of the bridge and, instead, we turn back in the direction we've come from. I make him promise to keep his legs in the kayak, not in the water.

My father is eager to continue kayaking, so we keep going to Holly Pond on the other side of Cove Island Park. I love seeing the expression of deep pleasure on his face as he paddles in the calmer water under the cloudless sky. We make it all the way around the island—a good forty-five-minute trip. My father is happy and full of vigor.

The next day, we head off on the same journey around the cove. This time the tide is lower and the water under Cove Island Bridge forms mini-rapids. A few spots require some navigating around rocks, nothing too challenging. Halfway across Holly Pond, I notice the water has become a little choppy, almost bubbly. Later, I learn that whirlpools form here when the incoming and outgoing waters of the tide meet and churn.

Once again, my father dangles his legs over each side of the kayak, as if he wants to simply float, as if some impulse I cannot see or fathom has made him pause right here, right now.

"No!" I shout.

Again, the kayak rolls to one side, and with a single splash he is in the water up to his neck. I paddle as fast as I can to him.

The water is too deep for him to stand in, and this time there is no place for leverage, no way to help him get back in the kayak. Instead, with his arms spread wide, he holds onto the front end of my kayak with one hand and to the stern of his kayak with the other hand while I paddle us backwards toward what proves to be an inhospitable rocky shore. My father is still in the water but at least with firm ground under his feet. I climb out of my kayak and reach out to give him a hand as he slowly maneuvers his way onto a flat rock, still keeping one hand on his kayak. We're both shaken, but we find a place to lodge the kayaks between some rocks. Taking a few moments to rest, we discuss what to do next.

I'm ready to ditch the kayaks and wave a passing boat for help. My father, however, is adamant that after a short breather we should paddle the rest of the way home. So that's what we do, climbing back into the kayaks, pushing off to make our way around the other side of the island.

The late afternoon sky has grown overcast and there is a slight chill in the air. My arms ache as we paddle into a rising wind. My father is ahead of me, his clothes soaking wet. I'm following, keeping an eye on him, on the weather, on the distance still ahead. Aware of pain and the gripping knot in my gut, I'm staying close to my anguish.

With each stroke of the paddle, I feel myself participating in something that has been set in motion. There is no turning back. We each have our own endurance. Mine has been tested today but I know I will follow my father's endurance wherever it leads us.

It's a long way back, but we make it.

Two days later, I'm home again. The phone rings: an old friend who now lives in California is calling out of the blue. It's been at least five years since she lived in Rhode Island; back then, we were both part of a weekly Authentic Movement peer group. Today, she's in the area for a quick visit and is having tea with another friend and colleague. She wonders if the three of us can seize the moment to get together in my studio. The timing is perfect: I had a morning meeting scheduled, but it was just cancelled. They arrive within fifteen minutes, and we make a plan for who will move and who will witness first.

I become a mover. My hands fly to the back of my neck and begin to shake with high intensity. I feel a sense of urgency. My attention, like a laser, is focused on the shaking of my hands. I don't know why this is happening but it feels important, something to stay with. I trust my hands and my body's instinct to shake and shed an internalized stress, but something more is going on. This place at the top of my spine is so specific, and the energy of the shaking feels driven in a purposeful way.

I learn later that during this time of meeting in practice with my two friends, my father is experiencing intense pain through his neck and arms. Over the course of the next few hours, the pain spreads through his whole body until ultimately, he cannot move and is taken to the hospital. My mother calls to tell me this as a surgical team prepares for an emergency operation to remove a dangerous bleeding hematoma. I get in the car and drive south.

Earlier in the day, the pain in his arms was blamed on the muscular strain of our two epic kayak adventures. No one is saying that now, but I cannot get this image out of my mind: my father submerged to his neck in water, arms outstretched, holding on to the ends of our two kayaks. How do I reconcile those days on the water with the horror I feel when, after his surgery, I see the raised red and stitched incision? In my mind, I see the wound descending from the base of his head down his upper spine superimposed on the memory-image of his outstretched arms. Sign of the cross. May there be healing within the suffering.

Would I have preferred if none of it had happened? Yes. If we had just stayed at his house, looking out at the water, watching others paddle or sail upon the sea? No. Sometimes we are compelled by a decision or act that is more choiceless than chosen. Sometimes we are in the stream of something greater than time. In such instances, the cause and effect meaning of "consequence" no longer applies. What comes to matter are the reverberations. And still, what most eludes my understanding is how timing expressed through *my* body interconnects with the impulses and actions of other people who are responding to a sense of right timing as it expresses through *their* bodies. Synchronicity is a high mystery.

These are dark days of despair. My mother and I are at the hospital constantly. My father's right side is non-functional. He will need to relearn how to use his right arm, relearn how to walk, how to move. He is discouraged, depressed, and on a cocktail of painkillers and meds. What more can be taken from a man who so deeply loves living life? First he lost the joys of taste, the pleasures of food and drink, then his voice, speaking and sharing conversations, and now his ability to move. At every step, he has worked his way back, regaining and reclaiming his powers in new ways. Each time full recovery becomes more improbable.

By evening of day two on the rehab floor, we notice a steady decline into confusion.

"We have to go," he pleads, "I have to get out of here."

Once again, we call it confusion, but what could be clearer when "here" is this body in pain, this body confined to a hospital bed, this body that's forgotten how to hold a spoon: *Let me be anywhere but here!*

My father's nighttime existential anguish comes tinged with suspicion: the nurses are again up to no good, danger lurks behind the curtains, and the light bulbs have turned into cameras. It occurs to me, as it did in the ICU in Boston, that I am witnessing an epic battle for the inner witness—for the presence of mind that knows what's real and what's not. When the confusion comes on, it seems we're in the realm of imagination but without the egoic-I to organize the linguistic and imagistic content. Random images, names, places, merge together, spoken with conviction as if they make sense, but it's like watching a boat adrift without rudder or captain to steer. Acceptance is a pretty tall order right now, and my father's having none of it.

"Let me out of here!" he cries, as my mother and I sit by helplessly. Nothing we do or say has any impact.

With perfect timing, Dr. Fred walks in the door. He is patient as he asks my father questions. He listens to his answers, takes him seriously, and then gently, firmly, reassures my father that everything will be okay. They will keep adjusting the drugs and physical therapy will help him gain strength.

"You will get out," Dr. Fred says to my father, "you will get home again."

The next day, back from the brink, my father is doing much better. Everything seems possible. The physical therapist is excellent, helping him experience good alignment before making any further moves. She knows all about the Alexander Technique and invites me to join her in working with my father. He is receptive and engaged. And his will to get through, even this, has returned.

Days go by, a week, and then two. My father discovers the hospital menu of alternative healing modalities: massage of various kinds, reflexology, and Reiki. One day I am with him when a young woman comes to his room. Her voice is soft and shy as she offers a hand massage. A gentle warmth quietly emanates from her. Just sitting near, I start to feel my own tension melt away as she silently takes each of my father's hands in hers with care and focused attention. Afterwards, he tells me how surprising it is that his whole body feels completely relaxed even though she only touched his hands.

Improvement continues day by day, his arms and legs remembering what they once knew. When he asks us to pick him up a cappuccino in the morning on our way to see him, we know he is feeling better.

More days pass. Sometimes at lunch he sends one of us out to get *linguine con tonno* or *salmone alla griglia* from his favorite Italian restaurant. Soon, we're told, he'll be able to go home, but he'll need round-the-clock support. My mother and I begin to figure out what we'll need to put in place for this to work.

We have a chance to practice when my father is granted a weekend day pass. Freedom! He's allowed to go home on Saturday and Sunday, so long as he's back at the hospital each evening. He'll be with us to celebrate my birthday. My brother John and his family are in town and join in the festivities. The rest of the family, farther afield, check in by phone.

After dinner on Sunday, my mother and I, as we did the night before, accompany my father back to the hospital. My mother finds a wheelchair, helps him into it and begins maneuvering him through the lobby while I park the car. I catch up to my parents and then it's just the three of us, rolling down the halls, slightly disoriented by the nighttime emptiness. After a few wrong turns we backtrack and locate the hospital map to find our way to an arrow that points to the rehab center.

We round the corner onto the downhill ramp of a passageway between the wing where we've been lost and the wing that is our destination. The wheelchair picks up speed. My mother, still strong and in charge, is running to keep up with the momentum of the chair. I grab on to help steer. My father seems unfazed by the speed—eager, apparently, to return to a place where he can lie down in peace and quiet. But for the moment, we feel exhilarated, swept up by a momentum we cannot control—the feeling of a caper.

Giddy with laughter and high spirits we barely make the turn, bursting into the area of the nurses' station. The first nurse we see is Germaine Fraser, another Authentic Movement friend, whom I have not seen in a long time. Greeting each other with smiles and hugs, we marvel at the miracle of her being here tonight, in a place she rarely works. Then we return to the business of getting my father back to his room.

After he is settled, my mother and I pass the nurses' station on our way out. Germaine is there and ready to take a fifteen-minute break. She walks us to our car as I recap my father's story and tell her we are looking for someone who can continue the rehab work when he comes home. She tells us she will help us find someone.

My father is full of energy, knowing he'll soon leave the hospital. He has been practicing specific ways to move with the walker and how to safely sit in a chair or sofa. I join him at the occupational therapy table where he is manipulating pennies into tubes and passageways. He is focused and seems to be enjoying the prowess with which he is accomplishing this simple task.

His physical therapist arrives and we talk. She says that when he approaches a chair, he tends to push aside the walker, getting his legs tangled in it as he falls backward onto the chair.

"This is unsafe," she tells us. "A fall would be devastating."

When she leaves, my father explains, "The problem is I'm always thinking that next time I'll do it right, so this time doesn't matter."

"Yes," I tell him, "I know that strategy well!"

I'm touched by his confession. It's a familiar quandary, yet another dimension of the unconscious will, and a twist on the question people have been asking since St. Paul humbly inquired in his letter to his friends in Rome: "Why, when I know what's right, do I do what's wrong?"

This was F. M. Alexander's same question when time and again he came up against his own propensity for habit. Even after figuring out the mechanics of anatomical motion, and knowing exactly what he *should* do, he discovered there was no guarantee that he wouldn't, in the moment of action, fall into a habitual pattern of response. His insight that the only way to override the power of habit is to seize the reins by paying attention while doing nothing became a central principle of the Alexander Technique. He called this practice of not-doing "inhibition" or "the creative pause"—a beat of emptiness, just enough to awaken a conscious choice.

The relationship between will and attention is at the heart of the Discipline of Authentic Movement. From the outset, a necessary degree of willingness brings us to this practice where surrender is always an invitation. The mover, with eyes closed, moves in front of a witness, not knowing what will happen, an act of trust and faith. And so it is with serious illness: the patient, so visible in this role to everyone they encounter, can never know what will happen next. I remember my father's note to himself: "Be generous, humorous, deeply supportive of all these fine people... be unself-conscious... take all the help you can get." How did he know, from the very beginning, that surrender was the first move?

We are now well beyond surrender. I've been thinking about what Janet has called "our core wound." There are moments in time that our deepest wound—everyone has one—seems to call to us. Reappearing in different guises, grabbing our attention, cracking us open, and ultimately initiating us into realms of deeper knowing. As I have grown older, I have come to recognize times when something extreme or unexpected happens to me as humbling experiences of sacrifice. I don't fully understand what this is, but I am learning something about it in relation to what my father is going through.

Janet once spoke about the relationship between sacrifice and intuition. When I asked her to say more, she shared her thoughts about intuitive knowing as direct experience:

> To ask to make a covenant with the moment
> requires letting go, letting go of everything that is
> not of this moment—deepening into everything
> that makes the moment. There is an infinite degree
> of detail one could become aware of. The gift and
> sacrifice are one.

And then she told me that the gift of consciousness requires sacrifice.

> The gift of intuitive knowing requires a sacrifice of
> all other ways of knowing, sacrifice of past expe-
> rience, and sacrifice even of one's own identity in
> order to become what one knows.

So, in the process of becoming and knowing more fully who we are, *the sacrifice and the gift are one.* Is this what I'm bearing witness to through my father's illness? Is it aspects of self—especially those parts we've most cultivated and most identified with—that must be sacrificed within the transformative process of becoming conscious of our innate wholeness?

Later, when we're back in his room, my father offers to share some of his lunch with me—soup, soft carrots, diced chicken bits with gravy, and vanilla pudding. I ask him if he ever gets sick of the hospital food.

"I'm not sick of anything," he answers. "I'm just sick."

Who is moving?
Who is witnessing?
I bow my head
you bow your head
separate and joined
in the mystery

TEN

My father is home. This is both a relief and a supreme challenge. My cousin Laurie and my father's cousin Gay have come from California to visit for a few days. They join my mother and me as we work to arrange equipment and caregivers needed for twenty-four-hour care. A hospital bed has been delivered and set up in the downstairs room, now dubbed the "Library Hotel." We've fashioned the couch into a bed for my mother so my parents can be together at night.

Germaine is coming to assist with the first evening's preparations and she's bringing her friend Mie, who has agreed to be part of our team. Tomorrow's morning shift will bring Deborah from a local home care agency, followed by Mie in the afternoon and evening. My brothers and I make plans to fill in when we can over the coming days and weeks. A schedule is taking shape, but we still have lots of gaps and there are so many unknowns.

One of my responsibilities is to help manage the pills—a complex and stressful task. Incredibly, the pill makers have created a system where the same drug comes in different shapes and colors, marked by different, minuscule letters for the abbreviated name and equally small, often faint, numbers for the dosage. Filling the week-long pillbox with its morning and afternoon cubicles for each day is a high-risk operation requiring constant double-checking. I cannot imagine how an elderly person could possibly do this without assistance from younger eyes.

Among other complications, my father has a potassium deficiency. The pills are too big for him to swallow whole, so he has to use a powdered version that tastes terribly bitter. I spoon the dose into a glass, stir in water, and watch the liquid turn bright orange. Standing close, I turn away as he drinks the fluorescent fluid that, in the high dosage he needs, cruelly burns his mouth and throat. In moments like this, I am both guardian and tormentor—an ambivalent custodian in the kingdom of pharmaceuticals, a realm I do not understand.

All I have is faith, trusting that the treatments are worth the pain and the humiliation of sickness that my father endures. The alternative, the likelihood that he probably would not have survived more than a few months past the original diagnosis, is too unbearable to consider. But it's not the drugs and medical interventions nor his strong will that keeps him here. He's not persevering simply for himself. He is doing it for the love and care of family and friends. And not necessarily in the context of survival, but in the forging of courage and fortitude.

Back in Rhode Island I wake in the pre-dawn dark, unable to sleep any more. My father is in my thoughts all the time now. I fear we may be entering a new phase, and there is so much we haven't said. Yet every time I think this, he surprises us with renewed energy. At lunchtime, I call to check in with my mother. She answers and immediately begins to sob, unable to speak.

When she can speak, she tells me, "Your father says he's done. No more treatment."

This is the turning point. The conversation we all knew was coming but didn't know how to broach. Instead, it has unfolded in its own time, led by my father. None of us has wanted to undermine the hope and determination he has displayed since the beginning. The family has been united in this—hope, love, and strength meeting hope, love, and strength. Over the coming weeks, I begin to see that this final surrender is not a failure of will but a further *relinquishing* of will. Acceptance is here; effort is gone. In this softening of will, as hope and strength fall away, what is left?

Love.

These are days to remember. Sitting with my father in the quiet with the birds and outdoor sounds, we hold hands or just sit near each other. Sometimes I watch or hold his jumpy feet. He always wants me to re-mind him of that word—*neuropathy*—"Oh yeah," he says with a resigned smile.

One day he tells a friend who has stopped by for a brief visit, "I've trained my feet so they're not so asleep, and I can walk better." He says it with a funny mix of pride and wonder. This inscrutable episode of the injury, spinal surgery, and rehab has been full of challenge and surprisingly, even grace. My father is learning to be more aware of his body and movement, as if learning something to take with him. Learning something new about being here. I think of Wendell Berry's "one-inch journey":

> And the world cannot be discovered by a journey of miles,
> no matter how long, but only by a spiritual journey, a journey
> of one inch, very arduous and humbling and joyful, by which
> we arrive at the ground at our feet, and learn to be at home.[22]

Sometimes, when my father is in the living room and I am passing through, he raises his arm, palm facing out. I raise mine and, across the space, our palms meet in silent greeting. Then one evening, he is sitting in his chair facing the water.

My mother calls from the kitchen, "What are you doing?"

He answers in a faraway voice, "I'm making my way to the front of the line."

Molly has decided to take a personal day off from work to visit her grandfather. Her cousin Maddie comes with her and the two of them take over the kitchen, baking and cooking their hearts out. While my father rests in the living room, I'm sitting at the kitchen table with my mother as she remembers living with my father in the early years of their marriage. She tells me that no matter how small and dingy their apartments were, there was always music, mostly jazz.

"I noticed," says my mother, "that your father had a special love for unusual voices. He always liked the men whose vocal range reached as high as a woman's and the women whose voices naturally went deep. He loves distinctiveness and the full range."

At one point, Molly brings my father a glass of water and sits with him as they look at family photo albums and listen to some of his favorite jazz singers. When I join my father and Molly in the living room, I see that he is helping her compile a list of his all-time great, need-to-know artists. On one of his notepads, he's written:

> Louis Armstrong
> Fats Waller
> Art Hodes
> Thelonious Monk
> Charlie Haden
> Hank Jones

In a separate column, he's writing down his favorite jazz singers:

> Nina Simone
> Alberta Hunter
> Billie Holiday
> Johnny Hartman
> Teri Thornton
> Esther Phillips
> Blossom Dearie

As he writes this last name, I realize that Blossom Dearie is playing in the background. Incredibly, I've never heard my father mention her before. With only a piano for accompaniment, she is singing "Someone to Watch Over Me," her voice embodying a tender and innocent longing, a pure, tender innocence. It makes me want to weep. *Tell me, where is the shepherd for this?*

That evening, I pick up a book of Rilke's poems and open to one called "To Music"[23] and read:

> ... O you the transformation
> of feelings into what?—:
> into audible landscape.
> You stranger: music. You heart-space
> grown out of us. The deepest space in us,
> which, rising, above us, forces its way out,—

The image of music manifesting as "heart-space grown out of us" stirs me deeply. Feelings transforming into mortality is the palpable landscape we are now letting ourselves move through. My father's presence becoming—more and more—simply love.

Opening my journal one morning, I see that I am running out of pages in the book. Running out of days in this life with my father. *Bob*—everyone calls him Bob. He loves to be called Bob.

Throughout this past week my father's brood—different combinations of his children and their spouses, his grandchildren, plus a few close friends—come by to see him. My mother helps orchestrate the short visits in between his increasingly long times of rest. I catch glimpses of some of these intimate encounters. Generally one or two people sitting with my father at a time. His gladness in seeing each person is an embrace, an honoring of their unique relationship with him.

One afternoon, my father is outside, stretched out on a chaise. Julia and I come to join him. She sits at the end of the chaise and I'm in a deck chair to the side. As I see my father and Julia talking together, I feel warmth in my heart, a gentle humming vibration. I become a witness, aware of an energetic space being created between and around them as they speak and listen to each other. I see Julia reach for my father's hand. They are holding hands as words and silence pass effortlessly between them. I close my eyes, resting in the quiet.

I can hardly stand to leave the house for the inevitable errands, but the day comes when my mother and I spend an afternoon going to local funeral parlors. My father is asleep on the sunporch as we leave so I ask Jeremy to sit with him while we're gone. I tell Jeremy that my father might sleep the whole time we're away so he may want to bring a book.

Later that day, Jeremy tells me about his time with my father. "It was just the two of us in the room for the whole time you were gone. I did bring a book but I couldn't read, I just wanted to sit there, taking him in."

"I'm so glad you were there," I say. "How was it to just be with him while he slept?"

"There was a feeling in the room," Jeremy replied. "And the sunlight was pouring in. I felt I was in a sacred space, almost like a chapel. Looking at him, I felt sad—I didn't know if I was ever going to see him again."

After a pause, he continued, "I began to wonder if watching him was intruding. Was I being a voyeur? When his eyes eventually opened and he saw me, he smiled and said, 'It's so nice to see you here. I'm sorry I haven't been very good company. I've been resting.'"

"He was so gracious when he woke up," Jeremy adds. "Greeting me in that way, the feeling that maybe I was being intrusive instantly disappeared."

Jeremy is sharing a memory from earlier in the day but his words are so evocative I start to feel that I am in the sunlit space of the sunporch with them. This is the kind of memory that I imagine will stay with both of us over the years, one out of which the felt-sense quality of the experience blossoms again and again. I then tell Jeremy how discouraged my mother and I were about our visit to the funeral parlors. There was nothing we found that felt anything like a sacred space. We are trying to figure out what will need to happen. There must be another way.

Later that week, two of our close family friends drive from Vermont to say goodbye to my father. They stay for lunch then leave in the afternoon. The next morning, one of them is back at the front door. He left Vermont in the dark to drive almost five hours to bring us a book. This time he stays for coffee, then drives home again.

I spend part of the afternoon reading the book. It describes options and legal considerations for what to do after someone dies—each state has its own laws. We know my father wants to be cremated, at least that was his thought when the prospect was more abstract. He and my mother have had recent conversations about all of this, but it feels so unreal. I still won't let myself envision his death.

Putting the book down, I step outside. A heron and three egrets are standing poised in the low, still water of Long Island Sound. Cicadas sing by the edge of the lawn, joined by the distant murmur of ceaseless highway traffic. It is just too hard to believe that soon my father won't be here to see the birds swoop before his eyes, or watch the big expanse of water slowly roll to and away from the shore, or hear the humming of the day—the bird call and train horn answer—or know the skinny dip feel of life as he sits gazing into the world's glory.

It's almost the end of August. I am in Rhode Island for two days to briefly catch up on the many moving parts of my life and belatedly celebrate Jeremy's birthday. On the phone with my mother today, she tells me that my father is sleeping a lot more. We talk about this like it's the weather, an update.

It is a strange and incomprehensible time. The day we are approaching is still ahead of us, still unknowable. So very reminiscent of the days leading up to the birth of each of my children; not knowing when it would happen was so unnerving.

My father is separating from us, beginning to be more elsewhere than here. But even from afar, here in the quiet, in the light through the window, through the green leaves, I sense a stillness within which our connection is alive and potent.

I return to my parents' house just as a truck is arriving to deliver oxygen. For the next few days, we help move my father and the rolling tank from the sleeping-at-night room to the looking-at-the-water room to the resting-on-the-sunporch room. Then the day comes when he stays in the library, mostly sleeping. One afternoon, my mother and I are sitting with him.

"This is hard," he says, his eyes still closed.

At first, we think he means dealing with cancer is hard. But then we realize he means dying is hard. How do you let go of a life that you've loved living? How does life simply cease its course through your limbs, your eyes, heart, brain, lungs, your hands, your body? How do you do it?

He sleeps again.

The hospice nurse tells us we should prepare for the end. The next day, John and Ben are here. Jeff is on his way. But again, my father surprises us, popping back in the late afternoon. Awake. As if, in the depths of his sleep state, he knows that his children are coming home, that soon we'll all be here. He asks for *The New York Times*, and says, "Isn't the US Open on?" We gather around the TV. We sit with him watching, not watching, talking, not talking. He is blowing kisses to us all.

The support of our caregivers, of neighbors and friends, is extraordinary. One couple brings us baskets of food every day for a week. The generosity of others frees us to stay close to my father, tending to his needs: pills, oxygen, morphine, washing, and just being with him. The focus of our little world of immediate family is completely centered on my father. The library room becomes a nest and my father, the opposite of a hatchling that we are each helping to care for.

Sam calls to say he wants to come back again to see his grandfather one more time. It is excruciating but I tell him not to come. I encourage him to let his last memory of Boppa be from his recent visit of two weeks ago when my father was able to engage in ways that were still familiar to us. I let Sam know we have the support of hospice and that between me, Ben, Jeff, John, and his grandmother, Mermer, one of us is always with Boppa, day and night.

"I'm so grateful he can be at home and that I am here," I say to Sam. And he tells me how lucky he feels to have had twenty years to spend with him, he just wishes he had realized it wouldn't last forever. When he says, "I'll never see him again, or speak to him, yet I know I will continue to learn from him," I burst into tears.

My mother, each of my three brothers, and I take turns in the library as my father lies in the portable bed. I sit on the couch next to him, watching the movement behind his closed eyes, his face still lit up by inner activity. Is it memory or thoughts or dream-states? What is he feeling?

Sitting right here, this close to my father, I can practically touch the unknowable. I feel so near to life as a threshold where the line between being here and not being here is disappearing.

Expressions flash across my father's face in the midst of experiences I cannot see, conversations I cannot hear. I bear witness, and sometimes I sing. There are not many songs I know by heart, but the two that come are "Home, Home on the Range," which was my father's favorite song to sing me when I was a child, and "Swing Low, Sweet Chariot."

Coming for to carry me home.

For two days I have not seen my father's eyes open or heard him speak. I am on the couch near him, in the quiet, when suddenly he sits up, eyes open, leans forward, and with great intensity asks,

"Where's my beer?"

"Your beer, you want a beer?"

"No, no, my BEAR!"

Later, it occurs to me that he may have meant the sea-green, soap-stone-carved bear, the one a dear friend sent him as an amulet in a pouch. It was a pouch into which my father had added other small, treasured gifts from friends. The same pouch that had accompanied him to treatment sessions and each surgery.

But in that place of closeness, in the blur between *here* and *not here*, "my bear," stands for something mysterious and essential. Without thinking, I say: "Oh Dad, you have such good guides."

And in this moment, I realize we are not alone. I know it like you know the warmth in the room where a fire is lit—an encircling sense of guardian presence.

His response is low and resonant: "I know."

These will be the last words I will ever hear my father speak. The way he says, *I know*, with a sort of quiet awe and appreciation will echo on and on. And on.

Exquisite morning light. Soft haze.

A bird passes through the calm doorway of water between two rocks.
May there be peace.

11:50 a.m.
holy, holy departure

ELEVEN

Forty thousand feet in the air, I'm both seated and suspended. Looking out the plane window at the puffy cloudscape below, I feel lighter, more defiant of gravity. I also feel disoriented. It's been a month since my father died. Yet he's still here. A silent, unseen presence.

I'm flying to British Columbia to spend a week deepening my study of the Discipline of Authentic Movement with Janet Adler. It turns out that the timing, planned over a year ago, is just right. After the long journey west, I pick up a rental car at Vancouver Airport, stop to buy five days' worth of groceries, and make my way to Stanley Park. I find a place to park that faces the harbor—water and fog, one undifferentiated wall of gray. Slow drops of rain are falling from the branches of a towering fir tree. Everything is falling slowly in my world as I feel raw, deep, lonely sorrow. I did not know grief could be so heavy, so wordless.

It takes a long time to do something simple like turn the key in the ignition. But once the engine starts, I know the next thing to do is drive. By evening, I am waiting for the boat to Galiano, a small island off the coast. In my seat by a window in the ferry terminal, it is too dark to see the rain, but I hear its steady fall. Behind me, on the other side of a shuttered kiosk, a group of men are watching *Hockey Night in Canada* on a TV hung from the ceiling. The sound is turned off; the men watch quietly, and when they lean closer to one another to share occasional comments, their voices are soft and low—the rain is louder than they are. I'm thankful for this public display of calm and peaceful camaraderie.

The next morning, I wake up in a small cottage wondering where I am. A band of sunlight beneath the half-closed window shade pulls me from dreams of my father: a series of close-ups, first his face, a smile, and finally his eyes looking at me. His eyes look away and then he's gone. I sit up, remembering the moments during the last weeks of his life when he or I would hold up a hand and the other would meet it, our hands briefly touching, long enough to feel the contact, the warmth of connection. My eyes fill with tears, as gratitude rises like a wave.

It's an easy walk down the road to where I will meet Janet in her studio space, designed and built by her husband Phil. Janet named her studio *the kiva*,[24] honoring the sacred structures built for ritual and ceremony as well as a pivotal time in her life.

I follow the path around a giant boulder and see Janet smiling and waving from the window. I stop to take everything in: the stepping stones embedded in the grass, the curved gray stucco wall, the little chimney on top of the sloping roof, the deep red flowers in a clay pot. I continue to the entrance.

It's good to see Janet again. Comfortable. Familiar. Here we are, standing together looking out at the swans that have just landed in the cove below. We talk briefly on the threshold, then we step inside the kiva. It is simple and stunning. The last time I was here, two years ago, it was a work in progress, a round concrete form, open to the sky. Four large empty spaces for windows faced north, south, east, and west, and eight small wall niches were set in the concrete. The rest of the space was left to imagine. Now the white plaster on the concrete walls looks like smooth fabric, the wood floor and trim around the windows feels warm and inviting. Eight beeswax candles are lit and stand in each niche. The space is prepared, ready to welcome all I bring.

For over an hour, I pour out the story of everything I remember since the morning my hands shook at the back of my neck, the same day as my father's surgery on the same part of his spine. After we look at several photos I've brought, Janet invites me to set them on the mantel above the fireplace. Then the time comes to stop speaking, to become a mover. I stand across from Janet. The circle of emptiness that lies between us feels full and potent. In the stillness of standing, my attention turns inward, enlivened by the simple, devotional attention of eye contact with my witness, my teacher.

Closing my eyes, I begin to walk, not knowing where I am going until I find myself at the curved wall by the entry. My hand presses into the surface, my whole body leans in too. Belly, side of cheek, and hands want to feel the smooth, cool whiteness of the wall. My body knows to find something solid that can meet me and support me in this cavernous feeling of sorrow, the sadness of knowing my father won't be here to share this next phase of my life.

I stay with the wall a long time before returning to open space, entering and following pool after pool of movement. Afterward, what stays with me is a gesture of my hands. One cupped hand fits into the cup of the other, not quite touching.

During our lunch break, Janet encourages me to take a kayak and paddle around the cove below the kiva. The water is calm, the blue sky, clear. I see some birds, a dog, a couple of sailors, and my father. He's everywhere here. I imagine him as a boy, canoeing on the lakes in Canada, paddling through wilderness, through nature's beauty. *See through my eyes,* he says.

I pull the kayak up the hill and return to the kiva, again entering the ritual practice of first moving and witnessing, then speaking and listening. Toward the end of the afternoon round of movement, a gesture stirs in my left hand. A small undulating form is beckoning.

Everything becomes very still and soundless.

> *Sense of being seen.*
>   *Sense of being seen by my father.*

Tears fall as a question forms: *What do you seek to see in me?*

Palms rise, opening.

I hear him say: *To see you offering yourself.*

A ringing bell marks the end of the moving and witnessing ritual. My eyes open slowly. I see the fireplace mantel where I placed the photographs. I see the photo of my father in his white terry cloth hat. He is smiling, his eyes warm and bright, his mouth slightly open as if we are in mid-conversation.

In the next photo, he and eight-year-old Julia are on a path in a forest of redwoods. They are walking hand in hand, their backs to me, the viewer. He wears a red raincoat, hers is blue. The vertical shape of the photo matches the vertical shape of the window next to it. The green in the image matches the green that fills the window space. Time is no longer stable. Time upends itself. I see my father accompanying Julia into the future, and I know he will be with each of the grandchildren, with all of us. I look again at the series of photos on the mantel:

Rectangles of time, windows into a timeless reality.

A new shape appears—a rectangle above me—a window to my father. I look up, seeing and being seen. The window is wide open.

I've already said good-bye to Janet and now, stepping outside the cottage one more time before packing up the car, I look out beyond the cove. The water is a darker reflection of the overcast sky, except where the sea meets the shore of a far-off island. A thin white line appears there, rimming the shore's edge, delineating the gray of land from the lighter gray of water.

The line separating one thing from another is rarely so clear. I feel myself crossing such a line as I put my bags into the car. Emerging from the deep descent of time in the kiva, the return has begun. The value of a retreat grows from just this—a separation in time and space from all that is familiar and routine. Even the unexpected calamities of day-to-day life are part and parcel of a way of being in the world that has little room for depth and mystery. The conscious shaping of time and space for retreat helps form the vessel for experiences to arise out of infinite time, boundless space.

Just as I turn my cell phone on for the first time since my arrival, it rings. Molly is calling. She's at work, on a break. She tells me how overwhelmed she feels by the long commute to her first post-college job in central New Jersey. She talks about her life in Hoboken, sharing an apartment with a roommate she feels no connection to and questioning her direction in life. And then—the tears finally come—how much she misses her grandfather.

I want to reach across the continent and give her a hug. I tell her about my kayak ride and how available and present he still feels, how much I trust that he is with her in some significant, if elusive, way. I tell her I have faith that she will find her own right path, and I tell her to hang in there, that the next step will become clear sooner or later. I don't tell her just how long it's taken me to learn to trust that each next step in life emerges in spite of my own uncertainty.

On the ferry crossing back to Vancouver, I stand on the deck watching Galiano recede into the distance. A few feet away, a seagull lands on a big metal box near the edge of the ship's side. In spite of attempting to perch there with dignity, the gull looks like a dog with its head out the window of a fast-moving car—half gulping, half dodging the wind that blows hard from the forward momentum of the boat. Suddenly the gull turns, surrendering itself to air—first falling, then flying. Are the seconds of free fall as thrilling for the bird as for the watching human? Something returns in me, a resiliency in the face of weight and gravity: forgotten joy!

When I get home, everything I'm not ready for is waiting for me. Julia is applying to colleges, Mariposa has started a new school year, and Jeremy is deeply involved with the new home project. Soon I will need to start cleaning out our house, getting it ready to sell. But first I need to go to Stamford to help my mother with the wrenching task of going through my father's closet and drawers.

Keep. Give away. Discard. My mother and I are bagging up my father's clothes in one of these three next-life categories. Whenever he found an article of clothing that embodied his ideal of soulful, yet practical apparel, my father bought multiples. The Norm Thompson short-sleeved Shikari shirt is the exemplar: a unique, casual version of the ubiquitous polo shirt. We find six different colors, most in duplicate. He liked jewelry—beads in his thirties and forties and a personalized Egyptian cartouche on a gold chain in his sixties and seventies—and hats, too. Nothing fancy or flamboyant: his favorite headwear was, for as long as any of us can remember, a white terry cloth cap fondly known as the towel hat. Again, we find multiples. The "keep" pile of my father's belongings for family members to look through is by far the largest, even though it's hard to imagine any of us wearing his clothes except in homage.

My mother and I take a lunch break and then go through his desk drawers and files. I look for anything that bears his handwritten script. Even simple to-do lists have a heightened charge. I discover an accordion-style folder filled with cards and letters. Inside, a yellowing envelope holds a series of typewritten notes I sent him in the early 1980s. The first note I pull out is typical of the vaguely aphoristic nature of my early writing:

> There was a time this past winter when I was
> walking to town a lot. For three days in a row, I
> passed a boy carrying a huge block of snow, plus his
> schoolbooks. In the spring, I saw him again. This
> time he was carrying a large chunk of wood.

A longer note suggests that my philosophic interest in the experience of time has been with me for many years:

> I have an odd sensation of my "potential future"
> jettisoning forward ahead of me. I can almost see
> it, but it's too much of a blur and I'm still standing
> here at this juncture of my life wondering if I will
> always have this feeling of something different and
> slightly unexpected about to happen.

> The real shock is not that the accumulating years
> add up to a particular age, but that our relationship
> to time is totally involuntary. It's like a beating
> heart, as long as we live, control is an illusion.
> Birthdays are a reminder of this.

These missives from my twenty-something self, remind me how much I trusted my father with my youthful and inward observations.

In another file, I find a letter from a young woman written in 1991, a year after she completed a fellowship at the company where my father worked. Like me, she took comfort in sharing her idealistic ruminations with him. She wrote about conversations they had about the role of women in the insurance industry. She remembered him telling her "how easy it is to just look and point fingers at the shortcomings, how much more difficult (it is) to be aware of the intricacies of the corporate culture, the limitations of people's abilities to work together (no matter what sex or what color), the internal political dynamics and the desire for market growth (with all of its own set of demands), and yet still try to accomplish a vision that is both just and contributes to the success of an organization."

A copy of his response is here, too, and, like her letter, the words are speaking to me now, fully relevant decades later:

> Most people, when forced to contemplate sig-
> nificant change, focus on what might go wrong,
> on what will be worse, rather than on what will
> be better. No change that promises less than
> perfection is acceptable, and since no change can
> promise perfection, change for the better is often
> not achieved. We seem to have a hard time remem-
> bering that one's grasp cannot exceed one's reach.

You can only ever attain what you reach for—another of my father's famil-iar mantras. At the same time, he understood the challenge of change because he knew the inner hindrances in himself so well. He knew that clear thinking can be undermined by doubt and cynicism; that shame and judgment shut down our feelings; and that fear derails our will. He knew that the problems in the world are, for the most part, neither technical nor simply the result of natural causes. They are sourced within ourselves.

My father worked in insurance, helping clients "manage risk," but his true vocation was his capacity to risk being his authentic self, which in turn encouraged others to be their authentic selves. I find, in another drawer, a speech he gave called "Risk in a Complex Society." The opening offers one of his self-deprecating observations designed to disarm his listeners but delivered, I have no doubt, with his characteristic humility:

> For you to understand what an intimidating
> assignment it is for me to stand here in front of
> you—the highest professional organization within
> our fine industry—it is necessary for me to confess
> to my woeful lack of formal professional insurance
> education.

Somehow, he figured out that the higher you reach, the more you need to know the ground you're on.

Back in Rhode Island, more drawers and cupboards await. I go from cleaning out my father's belongings to going through my own family's—beginning the process of emptying the house we've lived in for almost twenty years. As winter turns to spring, the days are a flurry of packing boxes, sorting treasure from trash. Preparing to move is a disorienting process of divestment that accentuates the weird convergence of time that I experience so often these days—past, present, future all blurring together.

One April morning, while walking on my favorite route along the ponds of Roger Williams Park, I realize, with a start, that I've been trudging blindly, head down, with barely any awareness of where I am. Looking up in an effort to stop the inner whir, I see the sun casting light through a gash in the clouds. That's the word that comes—*gash*—leaping inside me like something wild and hungry. Just ahead, a large branch has fallen from a tree and is lying broken by the side of the path. As I walk by, I see a gash in the trunk of the tree. Again, the word enlarges itself in me. I feel a gash in my heart and welcome it. Let it open me.

A month later, and there's no turning back. Within a week of putting the house on the market, we have a buyer who wants to move in by the beginning of May. But that's way too soon. We negotiate for a mid-June closing after Julia's high school graduation, but even that feels rushed. My days begin and end with the old familiar feeling of there being too much to do and not enough time. For weeks I have been telling anyone who will listen that I need a break. The writhing knot in my chest, when I zoom in on it, turns into a tiny figure with a giant, gaping mouth screaming: "I'm not ready!"

Ready or not, moving day arrives. Jeremy is en route to our new home in a packed car. He follows the moving truck piled full of furniture, rugs, and who knows what else we threw in boxes over the past few days. I am here in the house that still feels like home, even in its emptiness. Cleaning and gathering the last bits.

I carry some garbage out to the backyard bin, and on the way back I notice an old bird feeder that one of the kids made in elementary school. *Oh, we can't leave that behind!* I reach up to lift it off the giant metal *S* hook that hangs from the tree. *Ahh, got it!* As I turn to go in the house, it occurs to me that the unusually big hook might be useful at the new place. I turn back, then stand on my tiptoes, trying to get the hook off the branch; it's barely out of reach. I just need to get a little higher. *Ah, the bird feeder!* I put it on the ground and stand on it, my right hand extending up as far as I can reach.

Suddenly, feet fly up in front of me, my reaching arm flings back and for a millisecond, I'm lying on air...then falling fast. I land face up on the ground, my right wrist meeting a weatherworn piece of wood, one of the now broken sides of the decrepit bird feeder.

In the ambulance, the shock begins to wear off and I feel nothing but searing pain in my hand and wrist. Once at the hospital, I'm transferred to a gurney and wheeled into a hallway. While I'm parked here and left to my own devices for a few hours, the physical pain is joined by the too-muchness of the move, by everything—including my father's absence—that has happened too fast. I feel fragile and alone. Whatever it is that usually contains my sorrow has broken wide open. Nobody here to hold my hand, I am alone with my grief. As another hour passes, grief becomes my companion, so much more than a feeling. It is a fierce reality, both the passage I'm going through and the healing that accompanies me along the way. Grief is a thorny healer.

My new life begins with a broken wrist, surgery, and a bright orange arm cast. It's my lesson about reaching without paying attention to the ground you're on. Not what I had in mind when I declared that I needed a break. In the future, I intend to be more conscious about language especially when asking for something. And I pray this will be the last time I resist change by breaking a part of my body.

Through much of the next month I need to hold my bent, immobilized arm upright, to ward off painful swelling. I slowly unpack and put away clothes and books with my left hand. Family and friends seem to derive some amusement from silently joining me in this same gesture of the upheld right forearm, as if we are all members of some unidentified cult pledging our allegiance. It is a time of finally slowing down, resting, and healing.

We're in the country now. Our new home sits in a field surrounded by woods. Soon I'll be teaching the Discipline of Authentic Movement here in my studio. Each day by late afternoon, I allow my great fatigue to take me to a chair outside where I do nothing but watch the birds—mostly crows, gulls, hawks, and swallows—as they swoop and dive for insects and small critters living among the tall grasses, wildflowers, and weeds. I watch the sun rise over the eastern trees, and hours later, I watch it set beyond the western trees. Over the weeks, I'm amazed to see its simple arcing trajectory as the sun tracks north. In high summer, it will start tracking south again. Meanwhile, I give up trying to figure out what the moon is doing, appearing every night at unpredictable times in different parts of the sky.

presence
becoming
absence
becoming
presence

TWELVE

Hand hovers over heart, protecting but also revealing a tremulous question.

Can I really be open to a relationship with my father that transcends death?

For weeks after my father died, this question with its contours of sorrow and yearning lived as a feeling in my chest. One day, I knew the feeling was ready to move.

> My left hand slowly opens, palm soft and receptive
> something here in the cup of my hand
> elbow softens too
> a space is being created
> in the soft crook of my arm.

He arrives. His presence there beside me—aliveness and warmth all along my left side.

How do I know it's my father?

As I wonder this, the sense of his presence grows, as if in answer, as if he is saying *yes, I'm here.* And then there is no need to wonder, the direct experience is more than enough. A presence so large. Far bigger than the crook of my arm. He's here, and yet there is no actual sense of location.

I stay with this intuitive knowing as long as I can, and then what comes is the memory of being with him for the last time:

> Sitting on the couch, my mother next to me,
> both of us along my father's right side,

my three brothers across from us
on his other side.

The peace that has filled the room all morning deepens. All is quiet except the sound of his breath becoming slower.

And then,

an invisible point of light rising

What rises with my father's leaving is him disappearing, his presence now an absence, an absence that expands, filling the room and beyond.

Strangely, breath continues. Inhaling, exhaling, body still doing what it knows. But he's not there. For another almost minute, breath continues, no longer rhythmic, just in and out, in and out, mechanical. And then it stops.

I look at my father's watch on my wrist. Time stops, too.

We stay. We stay in the quiet of our own breathing. Left as we are here with the music, the beat and pulse of our mortal hearts.

* * *

Twelve months have passed since that last day with my father. Today marks a return and it also reinforces the reality of our growing distance. He seems much farther away compared to those first months when his absent presence was so tangible. Full circle and fast forward: two kinds of time. And now I'm living in a new home he will never see.

When I walk down our driveway to the mailbox, I pass the bench where he sat one summer evening, surrounded by a group of his grand-children, some strumming guitars. It was before we knew he was sick, when all that was here was a bench by a stone wall in an empty field.

Empty, but full of an extraordinary number of plants: Queen Anne's lace, Joe-pye weed, alfalfa, numerous varieties of clover and all the sweet-smelling grasses, offering food and shelter to the equally diverse number of buzzing insects and chirping birds, chipmunks, mice, and meadow voles. Now our human presence is here as well, with our house and studio at the north end of the field, along with our gardening and cultivating, our marking of seasonal change, our comings and goings, our gaze.

We planted a Japanese maple next to the bench where sometimes I stop and sit. The tree, still small, has begun to lean upwards into the open space where my father once stood. Even with the birdsong and breeze, this spot is an empty place. Time treats everything that never comes to pass as a kind of erasure, a deletion of what might have been. But on this day, exactly a year since my father's departure, I feel the call to find him as I walk back along the driveway to my studio.

Lighting a candle, I stare into the flame.

Memories awaken.

The room is peaceful
   standing beside my father, looking down at his body
      so still, beyond still

I take his watch off my wrist and lay it on a table
   I take my watch off his wrist and put it back on my wrist.

The previous weeks and even months had served as preparation for the simplicity of that final morning. Somehow, we were ready. In those last days, as he grew quieter, more still, there was nothing left to do but bear witness to his solitary leaving. Now, as I sit on the floor of my studio, watching sparks from the candle's flame, I feel far from that time. Today, every thought references a previous thought, an accumulating edifice of brain activity.

What else is here? What is ready to be moved?

Hands stir, resting near my knees. Sensitive to the texture of cloth, they slide along my legs. The *feeling* of movement obliterates any other thoughts, vanquishing them as illusions in the face of something real happening. Felt experience.

Attention widens, pushing new thoughts to the sidelines, following the parallel paths of each hand lifting off into space.

What is moving? What is forming?

Hands rising, palms orienting toward each other—tips of thumbs touch, tips of first fingers touch, forming a diamond window. The window opens into the emptiness of that last morning, and my father joins me.

Words for wordless knowing are hard to find. A fullness in my heart? An energetic, fluttery sense of nearness? Both. And a strong feeling of inclusion, a sense that this is not just for me. It is this sense of inclusion that I most recognize as my father—*all are welcome*—his expansive generosity. Here he is, his big open heart, here, right now. I feel his presence filling me and spreading beyond me.

And now fading. My hands touch down upon the floor. I feel the ground. *Here I am, found.*

It is in these moments of feeling my father's absence so acutely that some essence of him slips in. Here he is, out of all that is not sensory, not of this material world. Here is his presence. The tenor of the world changes as I feel the invitation to join him, to be joined by him.

In the space behind the candle, I lean three photos against the wall. In two of the photos, my father is a grown man, but in the third, he is a boy sitting with his younger brother, David, on the dunes of Lake Michigan. They are looking up at a cloud in the sky. It is a summer day, and even in the black-and-white photo, their shirtless backs look tan.

Both boys are leaning back, supported by their left hands. Three large glass jars full of blueberries sit on the sand behind them. David is pointing at the cloud; my father's right hand shields his eyes from the sun. The cloud is a small perfect oval hovering and slightly dark against the expanse of whiteness rising from the horizon line of the lake. And just above the cloud a darker band runs across the top of the picture.

The relaxed intimacy of this scene suggests it may have been my grandmother or grandfather who took the photo.[25] Their unseen presence, their view from behind the lens, is here too. And now, arriving from the future, here I am with my view, absorbing everything within the image that is speaking to me—the slope of the dunes, velvet smooth softness of sand, the space between the narrow-peaked evergreen trees growing so close to the shore. And that subtle, floating form, drawing attention to itself.

Looking over my father's shoulder when he is no more than ten years old—the photograph is like a relic that allows us to time-travel, taking us on the inward course of the contemplative gaze. When I follow my uncle's pointing finger, I hear that long-gone little cloud asking: *What is sky? What is dark? What is light?* The cloud invites us to look up. For me, this photo is a portal into timelessness where we can embody an experience of the unseen.

I think of my family—Jeremy and the children, my brothers and their families, my mother. And Dad, wherever he is, some place beyond but at the same time here with each of us. I see us earthbound ones looking up, like the boys on a summer day. The sky is so vast.

I look down at the flame. It grows large and sinewy with the breeze from the open doorway, then the sound of birds lifts my head again. I look out the studio window and see a hundred and more starlings fly into the top of a nearby tree. They disappear among the leaves so it seems as if it's the tree who chatters and sings. All at once the birds fly away and the tree falls silent.

That last summer, my father watched the birds with such focus and delight, following the flight of a gull, egret, or osprey until it vanished from sight. Even after the bird was gone, he would continue to stare into the empty sky.

I sometimes catch myself watching the sky, looking for my father, not yet ready for the emptiness. I see myself reaching. I see myself falling. Reaching and falling, this dance with fate where I strive and fail, seek and surrender. Intending one thing, I sustain another. I see myself reaching to find my father, falling once again. Finding myself.

At the end of the day, I return to the bench to sit as the setting sun turns the oak trees golden on the opposite side of the field. In the silent growing stillness, past, present, and future reside together here in the luminous glow of changing light.

More months pass. On New Year's Eve at a family gathering, we build a little fire from sticks, bits of bark, and dry needles, tossing slips of paper bearing something we're ready to let go of into the flames. For me it is the feeling that there is never enough time. I resolve to live with time more consciously, with more ease.

Starting the year fresh, I go through and cast off last year's magazines from the previous year. I find "The New Song,"[26] a poem by W.S. Merwin, with the line, "there is no time yet it grows less," and I realize that I am coming to accept this curious paradox.

A few days later, I'm looking out the window across the snowy field. An expansive kind of melding with the view is here. It's a way of being I remember feeling with my father, a way he had of taking in the beauty of the world without a trace of acquisitiveness. The feeling comes again that he is here, joining me. It comes as a welling in my chest, a feeling of pleasure tempered by...what is it? Sadness? Poignancy? Maybe he had an intuitive knowledge of impermanence, a resigned foresight that one day these sensuous, earthly pleasures would be no more. Perhaps he savored the fullness of life with some cognizance of the perishable nature of it all.

With sinking heart, I notice that these thoughts separate me from my father, eclipsing the palpable awareness of his presence. They take me away from the direct experience, the intuitive knowing, fleeting as it is, that we are not separated by a scrim of heaven or the weight of earth. In such timeless moments, we are together—until, once again, we're not. And still, I'm left with a clear knowing: *Now is the time to savor being in this body, in this life.*

In the quiet of the darkest hours of a winter's night, I awaken and make my way downstairs. Something compels me to pick up my journal from the year after my father died. I settle onto the couch, turning the pages. I'm struck by the absence of other people, by the lack of narrative, especially in contrast to the way I felt propelled through the eighteen months of my father's illness, carried along by a narrative that was writing itself. The after-year entailed a descent into an interior and dark passage.

In one journal entry, I am sitting outside attempting to write with my left hand because my writing hand, along with wrist and lower arm, is still in the orange cast. I note the summer breeze angling northward across the field, and the sunlight forking through heaps of cloud. My thoughts then turn to memories of my father, followed by "a brief, heightened interval" of feeling that I am experiencing the present moment as he might have:

> Sitting in a chair, one leg bent at the knee, foot
> resting on the knee of the other leg, I am looking
> up from a book, looking out at the sky, exactly as I
> had seen him do so many times. These memories
> of him blend with the shape of my own body. In
> this way that is both embodied and transcendent, I
> am sharing with him what is here right now.

The words drop me into a plumb line displacing any linear sense of time. Up and down, this is a verticality that feels infinite, a well that has no bottom.

It's still dark but almost dawn when I fall asleep on the couch. Waking a few hours later, I feel groggy and out of sorts. I stumble through the morning, wearing sunglasses in the house to foil the winter sun's sharp glare. Friends are coming for a dinner that needs to cook for hours. I sleep-chop the onions, carrots, the celery, and sleep-sear the meat. I sleep-shake the chili and slowly sleep-stir the pot. Soon I will nap before going on with the day.

I'm back in bed, about to fall asleep, when the phone rings. It's my mother, eager to tell me a dream, one so extraordinary she has to tell someone before she forgets.

"It was so vivid, realer than real," she says. "Your father and I were together. And the amazing thing is we manipulated time in such a way that we could be together."

"Tell me everything you remember," I say, now wide awake.

"I was in a huge stadium with masses of people and there he was, all the way across on the other side. We could see each other, our eyes made contact. Somehow, we managed to make our way through the crowd and find each other. Then we left the stadium. He was helping me pick out a bicycle and then we ate food together.

"But only he and I knew he was dead," she continues. "No one else could tell that he was anything but alive in body, sense, and soul."

She pauses, her voice almost whispering, "But here's the most important, most vivid thing of all. It was the way he looked at me from across the stadium. The glance, the same gaze I remember from the time I was eighteen—the 'Let's get out of here' look. The look that says, 'Let's be together, just us.'"

I wonder if this will make her sad.

"No, not at all," she says. "It really was real, it *is* real."

I tell my mother that while she was dreaming, I was awake in the night. We talk about the mystery of time. We talk about the mystery of life and death. And we talk about our favorite subject, my father.

Another year goes by. Once again on an early September morning, I remember my father, his passing and his presence, how he is in and with all that is good in my life. Reaching for a mason jar of seawater in the back of my refrigerator, I remember filling it from the side of the kayak while floating on Long Island Sound where we scattered my father's ashes. Today is the day I'm ready to empty the jar.

There's a place in the woods where a group of rocks mark the outer shape of a circle. I walk the circle, sprinkling water on stone, letting the memories return.

In my mind's eye I clearly see the eighteen kayaks, many borrowed from neighbors, lining the beach. Five of them are strewn with garlands and rose petals. A song is being sung—the words elude me now, but the hum of it is here as I move between the rocks.

The voices guide us—my mother, my brothers, and me—to our respective flower-laden kayaks, and then grow quiet. How silent the world becomes as we paddle, followed by the flotilla of spouses and children. Without words, in a kind of flowing synchrony, the five of us find the place to pause, floating, while the others glide into a wide circle around us. No other boats or even birds pass anywhere in sight while we all drift together, my father's most beloved circle.

I remember the night in France, when I dreamed and then awoke into the circle of twelve, of family holding and being held in a divine geometry of love, a constellation of light. We were at the beginning of my family's commitment to accompany my father. So much of that time was filled with darkness and challenge, grace and light, and the ever-present sense of not knowing where we were going.

Who would have chosen this journey? Life laughs at the question. No, the question was always: *Can you be present enough for this? And this? And now this?* To be present enough, this was the only choice.

At the end, it was a watery world we found ourselves in. There, on Long Island Sound, the circle became manifest. The water my father loved welcomed what remained from the burning—the last traces of his physical form. As slowly as I poured, the sea swallowed the ash. I couldn't slow how fast it all dissipated. Disappeared. Gone. Just gone. Then the surface of water closed up again—there was nothing more to pour.

The outer circle turned as each kayak slowly headed back to shore. Our inner circle floated in the still quiet for a few minutes more and then we too turned. I remember seeing my mother paddle forward, ahead of my brothers and me. She paddled alone, sitting tall, looking straight ahead to the shore. I saw her strength and sorrow, her spine strong enough to bear her broken heart.

Here in the woods, still with the memory of my mother returning home alone, I watch the last drops of water from the jar slide down the sloping side of the rock, disappearing into grass and weeds. When I close my eyes, I feel sorrow and strength rising within, and I see her sitting tall, her spine, a spiraling, shimmering column of light. High above her, distant beyond measure, is my father, a presence keeping pace with her as she continues on.

Something new is coming to me now, something I couldn't see before: my parents in the wholeness of their love for each other. Happily attached to my relationship with my father, I couldn't truly see my parents' relationship, distinct from my own daughterly needs and expectations. And now, with greater autonomy, I realize I no longer need them in the same way. Attachment gives way to more love. This, I know, is the beginning of preparing for my own eventual death. "We each have our turn," says Janet, acknowledging, in her heartening way, a simple truth of life. The sorrow I feel because of death has no end. My willingness to *feel* the sorrow, to open to all that death has to teach about life, is just beginning.

I take my watch from the drawer, looking at its frozen face and broken parts still held in the silver circle. The watch tells me it is always *now*. My thumb traces the circle, round and round. The twelve numbers, some visible, some imagined, are placeholders for this grand movement. As music is sound and silence, time is motion and stillness. It is the possibility of relationship in all directions, always returning, always evolving. Pathways of development more spiral than linear.

The timeless circle holds, in balance, the intimate center and the infinite periphery. It holds my father's vision of change: a movement toward the possibility of a larger sense of family, one that extends beyond the boundaries and bloodlines of kin. *Look beyond your own, take down walls, welcome others,* I hear him say.

Open windows, the night air. Frog music rises from the dark woods, heaving, vibratory, layered. The dark pond is dense with the voice of baritone beings, a thick hum rising through pond, field, woods, air, and human ears.

My hand reaches behind to the back of my neck, patting, finding a rhythm, a pulse, joining the thick hum. The place of wound is the place of knowing, the place of memory, the place of losing and finding. Emotion comes so readily now, such a delicate blend of grief and gratitude.

And the wonder of what continues, Dad—this bond between us.

Here I am
here you are
here we are
the same, different
still changing
within the timelessness
of life
evolving

AFTER

Markers in time are visible—the sun rising or setting. Or audible—the ticking of a watch, ringing of a bell, a first cry, a last breath. How necessary these markings are. They help us locate ourselves in the bordered domain of *this*, not yet *that*. The aftermath of death is so confounding because it is a remove from the visible. Yet, isn't most of life invisible? Our impulses, our feelings, our sensations, our intuitions, our past experiences, our future experiences all exist or have their source in the unseen. Perhaps time is a woven reality, a blending of the imperceptible with the manifest.

Still time has its way of moving on. Since my father's death, all three of my children have married and have begun to have children of their own. Other dear ones—friends, teachers, relatives—have also died. Mariposa closed its doors after ten years of providing early childhood learning to hundreds of children and cultivating community in collaboration with their families. With each passing, I light a candle and welcome again the sorrow and the inner stirring of questions—*what continues? what arises anew?* I am learning to notice and inhabit the slow unfolding of beginnings, the inexorable stream of endings. My body feels the flow of time, the current is alive.

During my father's illness, I struggled with the question of how to talk with him about the choices and mystery surrounding life, death, and the unknown beyond death. The process of writing this book emerged as a sort of posthumous conversation with my father. It also served as preparation for the summer of 2023 when Janet Adler died at the age of eighty-two. Janet spoke the following words in a film[27] released just a few weeks before her passing:

The part of me that is so used to doing is receding. A wondrous time, a wondrous way to enter life more fully at the exact same moment that I am feeling released toward my death.

Shortly before Janet's death, I spoke with her one last time when she was receiving end-of-life palliative care. After hanging up the phone I stood looking out a window for some time, held in the soft light.

Through the foggy mist and fading light of evening, I begin to see two forms moving slowly in the field. Two deer grazing. One is large with antlers, the other smaller, tawnier. The fog thickens as it lowers, hovering just above the grass. The deer disappear. I feel myself in a slow descent, tracking only what I can. *May I feel and see clearly what is here.*

Here I am within a vast, wide unknowing through which sorrow rises and falls. I am fine, I am utterly heartbroken. I see the deer again. They have reappeared some distance further away across the field. I am slowly crossing a field that is opening me beyond anything I know.

No longer contained within her distinctive body form, Janet's presence spreads everywhere. Here she is within memory, within that shape of cloud, that leaf falling, that clear cast of light on a floor beam, that wisp of wind, call of bird. *Pay attention*, comes the whisper. The invitation renewing itself again and again. *Witness the world in the details that speak to you and find yourself becoming more human, more yourself.*

From early on in her work, Janet knew intuitively that we need each other in order to awaken to ourselves. Her great offering to the world is this knowing—that the spark of relational recognition is how we remember who we are. Hidden within each human being, until awakened, is the capacity to be present.

Now, less and less does my story seem imperative, except perhaps in the hope that it will illuminate others' stories. How do *you* experience the enigma of relationship? Of life? Of death? What supports *you* in being present? What are *your* questions?

For me, new questions continually appear: How do we meet those who are coming into the world? How do we say goodbye to those who are leaving our "known" world? How do we stay connected to those who leave? How do we stay connected to those we leave?

Like so many questions we have barely begun to ask, these are, no doubt, unanswerable questions. But unanswerable questions are still worth asking. By not asking them we forfeit grace—we risk missing the glimmers, the visions, the unexpected signs. Perhaps the world is full of signs and intimations, and we miss them at every turn.

The watch my father wore in his final months of life was a personal sign placed directly in my hands. Another sign came to my family on the day of my father's memorial service. I have hesitated to write about this because it was not given to me alone. But now on the other side of my story, it appears as a bridge to new terrain where all of our stories mingle and meet.

It was after we returned from scattering my father's ashes, after we had left the kayaks on the small beach in back of my parents' home, and after gathering in the kitchen for plates of eggs, muffins, and fruit salad. We were starting to get on with the day. Some stayed in the kitchen, washing dishes and cleaning up. My brother Ben took a group of the cousins down to the beach to organize the return of kayaks to their respective owners in the neighborhood. Jeremy was sitting on the outdoor deck drinking coffee and chatting with my mother who was replanting pots of geraniums. I had gone to an upstairs bedroom along with Molly, where I asked her to read the eulogy notes I was preparing for the afternoon memorial service.

As Molly read my notes, I looked out the eastward-facing window, out over the water. An odd sight was just starting to register when I heard Jeremy call out, "Hey, look! What's that?"

About fifty yards away, a huge white bird was streaming toward shore in a direct line from the exact spot where we had scattered my father's ashes.

"It's a swan!" someone else called out.

Molly and I ran to the stairs and down, quickly joining everyone else coming from all directions toward Ben and the cousins on the beach. They were gathered in a row watching the swan come steadily closer with surprising speed, never deviating from its direct path. As we assembled, joining the other on-lookers, my mother, with her own flock of family to protect cried out: "Move away! Something strange is going on with that swan!"

"It's okay, Mermer," the grandchildren reassured her. "This swan is fine."

Emerging from the water onto the sand, the swan continued forward on its clear trajectory, stopping less than ten feet from where we stood on the beach. Starting at one end, the swan turned its gaze from one face to the next, all the way down the line. Slowly each person was held in this visual embrace until the swan reached the last family member. Then stillness.

Nothing moved, not time, not swan, not one of us.

The swan lowered its head, pecked at the sandy ground and stayed with us a little longer before turning to waddle slowly back to the water's edge. Pausing, the swan lifted its tail feathers into a wide fan waving side to side. An unmistakable farewell—or was it? One final gesture, emitting a solid deposit with a kerplunk onto the sand, sent us into gales of laughter. We watched as the swan slid into the water, moving with the same extraordinary speed, on the same straight path, back to the depths and out of our sight.

We continued staring at the water, longing to speak, longing to remain silent, before beginning to separate once again, each of us returning to what we'd been doing before the swan brought us together on the beach.

As the years go by, I occasionally ask members of my family what they remember of this uncanny visitation. Inevitably the details vary, but the memories usually include such qualities of the numinous as light, stillness, silence, timelessness, and the swan's more-than-swan presence. None of us imagined this majestic bird was literally Bob, and yet this extraordinary moment was filled with his presence.

This memory lives within me as an affirmation: all earthly beings are participating in something real, vastly larger and more intertwined than any of us can fathom. The unitive experience with my family and the swan tells me that we are each immeasurably more than our personal story. We are woven.

A book tells a story, a watch tells time. Until, as it happened, the hands of hours, minutes, seconds, fall away, and the numbers take flight—leaving nothing but the timeless grace of mystery.

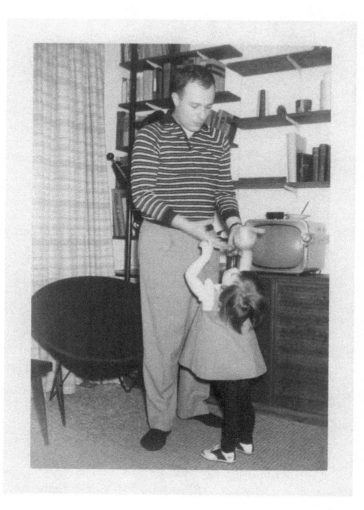

WITH GRATITUDE

I stand in the lineage of the Discipline of Authentic Movement which founder Janet Adler often described as a practice of embodied witness consciousness rooted in the traditions of dancers, healers, mystics. This is a stream that stretches back to ancient times, even as its current orients to the future. My gratitude for the support and inspiration of teachers, students, colleagues, and friends, likewise extends deep and wide.

The Watch opens with an epigraph: "I am who I am because of you..." In publishing this book, nothing could be truer. These words from Janet, so reminiscent of teachings shared with students over many years, were spoken in a recorded conversation with her friend Abbess Furyu Schroeder, just a few months before Janet died. Thank you to Abbess Fu, Rev. Dan Gudgel, and the San Francisco Zen Center for granting approval for the use of this quote.[27]

To my Mariposa co-founders Linda Atamian, Patti Smith, and Barbara Staples, I am grateful for the privilege of collaborating in that great experiment. My deep admiration goes to the devoted teachers and staff of Mariposa and to our executive director, Zoe McGrath. To each supporter and board member, a deep bow, with special thanks to Michael DeCataldo, Doris Gademan Stephens, and Marilyn Clements. To the children and families of Mariposa who trusted us, I will hold you always in my heart.

Between the lines and beneath the story of *The Watch*, lives the pulse and contributions of other communities of practice that have profoundly shaped and informed me: The Providence Waldorf Association; A Moving Journal; The Barfield School; The Center for Contemplative Mind in Society; and Circles of Four. I give thanks to all those—each one of you—who have participated and collaborated within each of these forward-looking initiatives.

For their invaluable suggestions, support, and close reading of an early draft, my humble appreciation to Hester Kaplan, Michael Stein, and Bonnie Morrissey. Thank you also to Jean Stone for her early editorial contributions, and to Scott Heim for bringing such care to the finishing touches of the final proof. Steph Turner's practical skills and creative contributions to my work, especially the digital parts, have been essential—my gratitude is boundless. And to those who have endorsed *The Watch*, I am moved and grateful for your generosity of time and witness.

For his support and special gift of intuitive hunches, I thank Jeff Genung for introducing me to Kate Sheehan Roach, my editor, trusted guide, champion, and now a dear friend. With Kate, everything is possible; without Kate, the manuscript would still be sitting on a shelf in my office. I am beyond grateful to her for reading *The Watch* and bringing it to Wesley Wildman and the intrepid Wildhouse Publishing team: David Rohr, line editor; Melody Stanford Martin, design; Ava O'Malley, Publicity Manager. Each and every one of you has been a dream to work with.

And finally, my family. . .

To Jeremy, forever my love—by my side through the living of this story and then again through the writing of it.

To Molly, Sam, and Julia, my great joys and earliest readers. Your continuing encouragement inspired me to keep going.

To my brothers, John, Jeff, and Ben—we went through it together, growing even closer—thank you for bringing the best of sisters into my life along with my dear nieces and nephews who each hold a sparkling place in the circle.

To my mother, whose strength is inspiring and whose support means everything.

And to my father, with me always—may his memory be for a blessing.

Endnotes

1. Edward Ardizzone, *Little Tim and the Brave Sea Captain* (London: Frances Lincoln Books, 2006), first published by Oxford University Press in 1936.

2. Janet Adler, "Suffering: A Personal Inquiry," in *Intimacy in Emptiness: An Evolution of Embodied Consciousness*, ed. Bonnie Morrissey and Paula Sager (Rochester, VT: Inner Traditions, 2022), 317.

3. Ibid, "Who is the Witness?," 81-101.

4. Wisława Szymborska, Nobel Lecture. December 7, 1996, Stockholm, Sweden: https://www.nobelprize.org/prizes/literature/1996/szymborska/lecture/

5. John Berger, *Bento's Sketchbook* (New York: Pantheon Books, 2011), 151.

6. Ibid, 156.

7. Tom Wolfe, *The Bonfire of the Vanities* (New York: Farrar, Straus & Giroux, 1987).

8. "The Child is father of the man" from William Wordsworth's poem "My Heart Leaps Up", also known as "The Rainbow" (first published in Part 2 of *Poems in Two Volumes* (London: Longman, Hurst, Rees, and Orms, 1807).

9. PA RT is an improvisational dance collaboration by Lisa Nelson and Steve Paxton, which they performed between 1978 and 2002. Lisa Nelson is a choreographer, improvisational performer, videographer, editor, publisher, and educator who has been exploring the role of the senses in the performance and observation of movement for nearly five decades. Steve Paxton (1939-2024) was an experimental dancer whose choreography was grounded in improvisation. He was an originating member of Judson Dance Theater (1962-64) and Grand Union (1970–76), and founding initiator of Contact Improvisation, a widely influential dance form.

10. Private Parts (recorded as an album in 1978) became the first and last episodes of Perfect Lives, a 1983 television opera in seven episodes (or acts) created by American composer Robert Ashley, directed by John Sanborn, and produced for The Kitchen, NYC in association with Fourth Channel, Great Britain.

11. Ingrid D. Rowland, *Giordano Bruno: Philosopher / Heretic* (New York: Farrar, Strauss and Giroux, 2008), 219.

12. Ibid, 219.

13. Giordano Bruno, *De Umbris Idearum*, (Paris: 1582) quoted in Hilary Gatti, *Essays on Giordano Bruno* (Princeton, NJ: Princeton University Press, 2011), 212.

14. Arthur Zajonc, *Meditation as Contemplative Inquiry: When Knowing Becomes Love* (Great Barrington, MA: Lindisfarne Books, 2009).

15. Simone Weil, *Gravity and Grace* (Nebraska: Bison Books, 1997), 45.

16. Art Hodes and Chadwick Hansen, *Hot Man: The Life of Art Hodes* (Illinois: University of Illinois Press, 1992), 28.

17. Georg Kühlewind, *Wilt Thou Be Made Whole?: Healing in the Gospels* (Great Barrington, MA: Lindisfarne Books, 2008), 57.

18. Gertrude Hughes, *More Radiant than the Sun: A Handbook for Working with Steiner's Meditations and Exercises* (Great Barrington, MA: SteinerBooks, 2013).

19. Langston Hughes, "Island," in *Selected Poems of Langston Hughes* (New York: Vintage Classics, 1959).

20. Robert Frost, "Mending Wall," in *North of Boston* (London: David Nutt, 1914).

21. Henry Miller, *Tropic of Capricorn* (New York: Grove Press, 1961), 170. Originally published in Paris by Obelisk Press-Seurat Editions, 1939.

22. Wendell Berry, *The Unforeseen Wilderness: Kentucky's Red River Gorge* (Berkeley, CA: Counterpoint, 2007, originally published by The University of Kentucky Press in 1971), 43.

23. Rainer Maria Rilke, excerpt from "To Music," from *New Poems* (1907, 1908) in *Ahead of All Parting: The Selected Poetry and Prose of Rainer Maria Rilke*, edited and translated by Stephen Mitchell (New York: Random House Modern Library Edition, 1995), 143.

24. In the early 1980s, Janet found refuge and welcome from the Huichol people in Sedona, AZ. There, Janet worked with Jaichima, a Huichol shaman originally from the Wirarika tribe in central Mexico. In 2012, after Jaichima transitioned, her brother Rutury, also a shaman who worked closely with his sister for forty years, continued to carry on her legacy. From Rutury, Janet received his blessing of her naming of her teaching space. (See *Intimacy in Emptiness: An Evolution of Embodied Consciousness*, 185.)

25. The photograph of my father and uncle, likely taken in the early 1940s, appears as the frontispiece of this book.

26. W.S. Merwin, from "The New Song" in *The Moon Before Morning* (Port Townsend, WA: Copper Canyon Press, 2014).

27. Janet Adler in dialogue with Green Gulch Farm Abiding Abbess Furyu Schroeder during the online event, "The Collective Body as Sangha," hosted by Paula Sager and Bonnie Morrissey and produced by the San Francisco Zen Center on November 12, 2022. (Available on YouTube *https://www.youtube.com/watch?v=CYcr8BhJOVY*)

Paula Sager is a writer and teacher of somatic and contemplative practices. Beginning her career as a dancer and choreographer, she became certified as a teacher of the Alexander Technique, followed by decades of immersive work with Janet Adler, a revered pioneer of embodied witness consciousness. Paula is a faculty member of Circles of Four, a teacher training program in the Discipline of Authentic Movement. She holds a BA in Dance from Bennington College and an MA from the Barfield School at Sunbridge College, where her research focused on the development of the inner witness. Paula served as founding co-editor of *A Moving Journal* from 1994-2006 and is co-author with Lizbeth Hamlin of *Red Thread, Two Women* (Pacific Editions), a long-distance experiment in moving, witnessing, and word, designed by book artist Charles Hobson. In collaboration with Janet Adler, Paula Sager and Bonnie Morrissey coedited Janet's collected writings, *Intimacy in Emptiness: An Evolution of Embodied Consciousness* (Inner Traditions).